Two Plays

THE LIAR
THE ILLUSION

First published in 1989 by Absolute Classics, an imprint of
Absolute Press, 14 Widcombe Crescent, Bath, England

Series Editor: Giles Croft

Cover and text design: Ian Middleton

Photoset and printed by WBC Print, Bristol

ISBN 0 948230 22 3

THE LIAR
THE ILLUSION

Two plays by

Pierre Corneille

Translated and Adapted by Ranjit Bolt

absolute classics

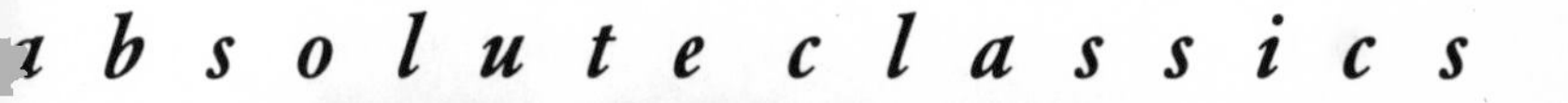

FOR SHERIDAN FRANCE

INTRODUCTION

In later life, Corneille the august tragedian seems to have regretted his boisterous, comic beginnings, and even to have revised his early work in an effort to uncover a vein of *dignitas*. It seems to me that his misgivings were misplaced. Of course, the comedies make no attempt to tackle "lofty themes". But is it not the very shamelessness (and sure-footedness) with which they eschew such themes that gives them their charm? To a layman, raised on LEAR and HAMLET, watching French tragedy can be a puzzling experience. The protagonists are clearly upset about something. Pretty soon, and often with soporific consequences, we learn what it is that they are upset about. But as to why they are upset - or rather, why they *should* be upset - we are all too often left in the dark. Yet experts assure us that this is high art. That the comparison of Racine with Shakespeare is a legitimate critical exercise. Even that the resulting contest, if such it be, is more or less equal. I cannot help thinking that Cornelian comedy survives such a trial by contrast, if not unscathed, at any rate less severely mauled!

Finally, a word on these versions. With LE MENTEUR I have taken one or two liberties - fair enough, perhaps, as it was itself more or less an adaptation. Corneille's menials are not very clearly differentiated, either in speech or characterisation, from their masters and mistresses. It was this that prompted the excision of Isabelle, Clarice's maid, and the transfer of her lines to Lucrèce. In addition, one or two speeches have been moved, and about a dozen lines of my own inserted. Argante's stammer is another invention of mine - forgiveable, I hope. As for L'ILLUSION, I have remained very faithful to the original. The piece seems to me so wonderfully weird as to defy alteration.

RANJIT BOLT

THE LIAR

CHARACTERS

GERONTE (Dorante's father)

ARGANTE (Citizen of Poitiers and friend of Géronte)

DORANTE (Géronte's son)

ALCIPPE (An old friend of Dorante's, and Clarice's fiancé)

PHILISTE (Friend of Dorante and Alcippe)

CLARICE (Alcippe's fiancée)

LUCRECE (Clarice's friend and confidante)

SABINE (Lucrèce's maid)

CLITON (Dorante's valet)

LYCAS (Alcippe's valet)

ACT ONE

The Tuileries gardens.
Dorante, Cliton.

DORANTE: I've swapped my gown for what I've always wanted –
A sword. At last, Cliton, my father's granted
My dearest wish: I've finished with the law
And all its works – let's drink a toast to war!
But tell me, since we're in the Tuileries –
A place that throbs with style and gallantry –
Am I cut out to play the cavalier,
Or am I still too scholarly? I fear
The finer points of Tort and Contract may
Have left me permanently démodé.

CLITON: Monsieur Dorante! Law wasn't your vocation;
You're built for quite a different occupation –
That walk, those looks – they're hardly what I'd call
Scholarly. No, you ought to channel all
Your energies into seducing women –
Husbands've got a lot of trouble coming.
D'you like it here?

DORANTE: This city is a jewel –
My studious exile seems all the more cruel.
But you're my valet – I'm expecting you
To find me some amusing things to do.
Tell me, for instance, how should I deport
Myself with women?

CLITON: That's the favourite sport
With cavaliers. But what an appetite!
(If I may say so) – you arrived last night,
And here you are, already primed and cocked
For amorous action – why, I'm almost shocked.
Still, if that's what you're after, I'm your man –
I can oblige, if anybody can:
I'm quite an expert in the pimping art –
At any rate, there's no one in this part
Of town to touch me.

DORANTE: I don't want a whore!
I'm looking for amusement, nothing more –

A girl in whose delightful company
The tedious hours will pass more pleasantly. . . .
Somebody I can flirt with now and then.

CLITON: I'm with you now, you're not one of those men
Who only like a woman if she's paid for.
But, there again, you weren't exactly made for
Insipid chats with innocent coquettes:
Some sultry looks are all a lover gets
From that pernicious breed - why waste your time
On the ridiculous, with the sublime
Staring you in the face? I mean, of course,
Those wealthy ladies whose behaviour's worse
Than "etiquette" demands - though mainly chaste,
They don't mind sinning, if it's done with taste.
But why ask me about it? You don't look
As though your nose was always in a book
And never got a chance to . . . sniff the air.

DORANTE: What perspicacity! I've sown my share
Of oats, it's true - but Paris and Poitiers
Are a long way apart, and I dare say
They call for very different strategies.
Provincial women aren't that hard to please:
Men are considered eligible there
Who wouldn't have a hope in Hell up here.
Just look around - this city is awash
With bright young things, eager to cut a dash.
The social stakes are high - unless you hold
Some decent cards, you may as well just fold.

CLITON: Study the facts before you judge the case:
Paris is an enormous market-place;
Not all the merchandise is genuine,
And people are quite often taken in.
For every dazzling wit with three degrees
You'll find a dozen mediocrities.
People arrive here from all over France,
And half of them are frauds, wanting the chance
To make a fresh start, build a reputation,
And rise in other people's estimation
The way they've long since risen in their own.
A lot of good-for-nothings have been known
To prosper here. But let's return to what

We were discussing: I assume you're not
Tight-fisted?

DORANTE: No.

CLITON: That's good: an open palm
In matters of the heart'll do no harm.
But when you're spending, show a bit of taste,
Or all your hard-earned cash'll go to waste.
Gifts are important, yes – but so's the way
They're given, if you want to make them pay:
Some lovers lose at cards deliberately,
Or leave a necklace lying about, that she
Would rather die than wear – presents like these
Disgust the mistresses they're meant to please.

Conversation of ladies, drawing nearer.

DORANTE: Enough – I don't concern myself with churls.
But tell me, who are those delightful girls?

CLITON: I couldn't say. I thought I'd made it clear:
I operate in quite a different sphere.
But don't despair, I'll ask their coachman – he
Should give me details of their pedigree.

Exit.

As Clarice and Lucrèce enter, Dorante stands aside to eavesdrop.

CLARICE: I can't help thinking that the Tuileries
Isn't as pleasant as it used to be:
One's scarcely gone a step before some fop
Attempts to flirt with one – they seem to drop
Out of the trees like rotten fruit.

LUCRECE: Agreed.
Some decent poetry is all *I* need
To keep me occupied – and as for you
You're spoken for – the last thing you should do
Is let yourself be seen with other men.
Alcippe will be your husband soon.

CLARICE: But when?
A while ago his father went to Tours,
And now there seems to be an endless store
Of reasons why he can't come back – the roads –

His health – the time of year – which hardly bodes
Well, and each time the wedding is delayed
I see myself dying a rich old maid!
You don't score points, playing the waiting game,
If what begins as loyalty ends in shame.

LUCRECE: If you reject Alcippe, where will you find
Another man who suits your turn of mind?

CLARICE: I won't dispense with him until I've found
The right replacement – I'll be on safe ground
Throughout. The old man can't have gone for good –
I'd rather have Alcippe than spinsterhood!

DORANTE: *(Aside)* I'm out of touch, all right! So this is how
Ladies of fashion talk in Paris now!

At this point Clarice looks down and sees that one of her shoe laces is undone.

CLARICE: These wretched shoes!

DORANTE: Madame, allow me, please –
I'm just the man for these extremities!
Heaven be thanked for sending this excuse
To talk to you and make myself of use.

He bends down and ties the lace.

CLARICE: Heaven has more important things to do
Than supervise the lacing of a shoe.

DORANTE: You're right, of course – I owe this all to chance –
A fortunate but random circumstance,
Neither contrived by me, nor, I'm afraid
Desired by you – my joy begins to fade.

CLARICE: How rapidly your ecstasies abate!
Allow me to play devil's advocate:
Good fortune's twice as welcome, I believe,
When undeserved, just as we don't receive
A debt repaid with half the eagerness
We do a gift. A favour won't impress
If it's an old one merely being returned –
Nor does good fortune, when we feel it's earned.
A stroke of luck will bring us, without pain,
What years of diligence could not obtain.

DORANTE: Make no mistake, I'm only too aware
How far I am from meriting so rare
A privilege as this: my amorous heart
Appreciates the lapse on Fortune's part.
It would be beating even faster, though,
Had you in fact intended to bestow
This honour: lovers cannot be content
With favours granted them by accident.
What I've been saying really all amounts
To one old proverb: it's the thought that counts.
Suppose a woman gives a man her hand,
But keeps her heart – love's flames are scarcely fanned
At all. I take your hand – I kiss it *(Kisses it.)* – yet
Why bother, when your heart's so hard to get?

CLARICE: These flames of yours, monsieur, are news to me –
It seems I've caught them in their infancy
You're highly flammable, I must say – my
Romantic tinder isn't half so dry.
However, now that you've alerted me,
Perhaps I'll view them with more sympathy
In time – but no more tales of love rejected:
Love can't be spurned before it's been detected.

Cliton returns.

CLITON: *(To Dorante.)* The coachman says. . . .

DORANTE: *(To Cliton.)* Not now, Cliton. *(To Clarice.)* It seems,
I'll have to set aside my amorous schemes.
I'm not surprised: bad luck's been dogging me
Ever since my return from Germany,
Which must've been at least a year ago –
I was on active service there, you know.
I swear, I've scarcely left your part of town
In all that time: I've sought you up and down –
You've been my guiding light – my eastern star –
Hitherto I've admired you from afar,
But some . . . daemonic influence today
Forces me to declare my love.

CLARICE: You say
You fought in Germany?

DORANTE: I was the chap
They used to call "The Human Thunderclap".

CLITON: *(Aside)* What is he on about?

DORANTE: The things I've done!
Scarcely a siege was raised, a battle won,
In which I didn't have my share of glory –
My name was mentioned. . . .

CLITON: *(Aside to Dorante, in a whisper.)*What's this crazy story?

DORANTE: Shut up!

CLITON: You're mad!

DORANTE: Shut *up*!!

CLITON: *(Shaking him.)* You're from Poitiers,
Remember? You arrived here yesterday.

DORANTE: For the last time, SHUT UP!!! As I was saying,
I've done my share of pillaging and slaying,
And I would like to think my reputation
Was earned.

CLARICE: Why quit this glorious vocation?

DORANTE: Last winter I returned in order to. . . .
Attend at court . . . that's where I first saw you.
I came, I saw, you conquered: your sweet charms
Left me no choice but to lay down my arms.
Here – take my heart and soul – I must surrender,
Lock, stock and barrel to your beauty's splendour.
Once I commanded men – now here I stand,
Among love's other ranks, yours to command.
What do I care for victories and fame?
To serve you faithfully is my sole aim.

LUCRECE: *(In a whisper to Clarice.)*
Don't look now, but Alcippe's coming this way –
I think there might be trouble if we stay.

CLARICE: *(To Dorante.)* Sir, I've enjoyed our talk, but I'm afraid
Your vassaldom may have to be delayed.
Goodbye.

DORANTE: But you're my reason for existence!

CLARICE: Look, flattered though I am by your persistence,
I simply haven't time to stop and talk –
My friend and I are going for a walk.

DORANTE: Since you're the inspiration for my love,
Just condescend to say if you approve.

CLARICE: I shouldn't need to, judging from your tone:
True love requires no licence but its own.

Exeunt ladies.

DORANTE: Well, don't just stand there – follow them!

CLITON: What for?
The ladies' coachman couldn't have been more
Co-operative: "A tasty little piece,"
He says, "I work for her – her name's Lucrèce.
They both live in the Place. . . ."

DORANTE: The Place?

CLITON: THE Place –
The Place Royale. As for the plainer face,
He couldn't put a name to it, but I
Could probably find out.

DORANTE: Don't bother.

CLITON: Why?

DORANTE: Lucrèce has claimed my heart – Lucrèce must be
That captivating girl who spoke with me.
"A tasty piece," he said – well, that was her,
I'm certain of it.

CLITON: As your valet, sir,
I shouldn't disagree, but in my view
The other one's the prettier of the two.

DORANTE: That standing stone?! That mute, who couldn't find
Three words to let you know she had a mind?!

CLITON: Ah, but a girl with nothing much to say's
A rarity – a miracle – these days,
And should be prized. I'm a straightforward man –
I take my pleasures when and where I can –
An opportunist, not romantically
Inclined at all; but if I chance to see
A girl just sit there, absolutely mum,
For hours on end, I'm liable to succumb:
Beautiful women should be seen, not heard.

That's why the one who didn't say a word
Is bound to be Lucrèce.

DORANTE: This homily
Has gone on long enough. *(Looking off.)* What's this I see?
Alcippe! Philiste! Two of my dearest friends –
They'll be amazed to see me here again . . .

Dorante and Cliton stand aside as Alcippe and Philiste enter.

ALCIPPE: Music and food?

PHILISTE: "*Collation et musique.*"

ALCIPPE: On water?

PHILISTE: "*Sur l'eau.*"

ALCIPPE: Pleasant?

PHILISTE: "*Magnifique.*"

ALCIPPE: Last night, you say? Who gave it?

PHILISTE: I don't know.
I wasn't there.

DORANTE: Ehem!

ALCIPPE: Dorante! Hello!!
Come here, old friend!

They embrace.

DORANTE: Sorry to interrupt –
It was my joy that made me so abrupt.

PHILISTE: Of course! Come here!

They embrace.

DORANTE: What were you speaking of?

ALCIPPE: Nothing important. It's to do with love.

PHILISTE: A sort of music party that some beau
Gave for a lady.

DORANTE: On the Seine?

ALCIPPE: "*Sur l'eau.*"

DORANTE: It's a strange thing, but waves can sometimes fan
The flames of love.

PHILISTE: *(Frowning as he tries to sort out the metaphor.)*
Waves can't fan flames.

DORANTE: They can.
Last night, this party, was it?

ALCIPPE: Yes, that's right.

DORANTE: Love's flames become more visible at night.
But what about the lady – was she worth
The effort?

ALCIPPE: *(From the heart.)* She's the loveliest girl on earth.

DORANTE: How was the music?

PHILISTE: I believe, so-so.

DORANTE: And supper?

PHILISTE: Pretty good, as suppers go.

DORANTE: *(Starting to chuckle.)*
I see. Presumably you know whose money
Paid for all this?

ALCIPPE: Not yet. But what's so funny?

DORANTE: What's funny is that I'm the man who threw
This splendid party. . . .

ALCIPPE: What?!

PHILISTE: You don't mean?

ALCIPPE: *(Accusingly)* You!!

DORANTE: Me.

ALCIPPE: *(Bitterly)* You've already found a mistress, then?

DORANTE: Hardly a feat of dazzling prowess, when
You think it's several weeks since I arrived.
For various pressing reasons, though, I've lived
In semi-isolation, only free to
Step out of doors at night, and incognito.
But the nocturnal visits I've been paying
To a particular. . . .

CLITON: *(To Dorante, aside.)*
What *are* you saying?!

DORANTE: *(To Cliton.)*
I've told you once, I don't need your advice.

CLITON: I can't stand by and listen to these lies.

ALCIPPE: *(To Philiste.)* Dorante's my rival, then!

PHILISTE: *(To Alcippe.)* How fortunate
We met him when we did.

DORANTE: Let me relate
The details of the party to you, friends:
In order to attain my amorous ends
I hired five boats; in four of them I placed
Musicians – ah! their playing would have chased
The blackest cares away – in one boat, flutes;
In the next, violins; in the third, lutes
And voices; oboes in the fourth. They played
In turns, and let sweet melodies pervade
The evening air. Behind them came a barge –
A lattice-work of foliage was its charge,
Designed to freshen up the atmosphere,
With oranges and jasmine here and there,
And pomegranates, mingling their sweet scents.
This was to be the centre of events,
And here the girl on whom my hopes depend
Was brought, with five more beauties to attend
On her. The dinner followed straightaway.
I won't go into detail . . . let's just say
There were six courses, and in every course
A dozen dishes. While, to reinforce
My orchestras, rocks, waves and winds combined
In echoing harmony. After we'd dined
Thousands of fireworks shot into the sky –
All shapes and sizes, dazzling the eye
With fiery trains – a flood of flame that streamed
Into the water – why, it almost seemed
As though two elements, sworn enemies
Were locked in strife before our very eyes,
And night had turned to day! Well, after this
We danced, till day broke, cutting short our bliss.

ALCIPPE: *(In torment by now.)*
A stylish narrative. It must have been
A ball the like of which is rarely seen
Even in Paris.

DORANTE: Just a small affair –
Two hours was all she gave me to prepare.

PHILISTE: And yet, a great deal of expense and thought
Went into it. . . .?

DORANTE: *(Blasé)* Philiste, when time is short
One simply does the best one can.

PHILISTE: No doubt.

ALCIPPE: Look, this is something we must talk about
When I've more time.

DORANTE: You can depend on me.

ALCIPPE: Goodbye, then.
(To Philiste as they go.) I'm half dead with jealousy!

PHILISTE: You've got no cause to be – scarcely a word
Of his account agreed with what I'd heard.

ALCIPPE: The time and place do – that's enough to shatter
My hopes forever – what do details matter?

Exeunt Alcippe and Philiste.

CLITON: Is it alright if I speak openly?

DORANTE: When we're alone, yes – not in company.

CLITON: You've got a curious urge – or so it seems –
Correct me if I'm wrong – to talk in dreams.

DORANTE: In dreams?

CLITON: Since you're my master, sir, I'm trying
To be discreet – others might call it lying.

DORANTE: Your wits are addled.

CLITON: If they are, the cause
Is all this talk of orchestras and wars.
You've fought in countries that you've never seen
And given balls that didn't cost a bean!
You told that girl you'd been in town a year!

DORANTE: I had to make my passion look sincere.

CLITON: But what have battles got to do with love?

DORANTE: Do you imagine that it would improve
My chances if I said to her: "Madame,
My fate is in your hands - what's more, I *am*
A qualified lawyer - if you need advice
It's yours for free. I've mastered all the nice
Distinctions between Digests Old and New,
And quite a lot of Jurisprudence too.
My legal prowess is at your disposal."
Of course, she'd be enthralled by *that* proposal!
These proud, disdainful beauties secretly
Long for a lover with a law degree!
Some learned languishing, that's what they want:
The Prince of Precedents - what a gallant!
Don't make me laugh, Cliton - a martial manner
Is what's required: just slip in, when you can, a
Grimace or two, a daring oath, a lie,
A little jargon, the odd victory,
A fortress with a funny-sounding name -
To fascinate and thrill should be your aim.
Watchtowers and trenches, battle plans, designs,
Earthworks and counterscarps, angles and lines -
Mix it all up and throw it in the pot,
And though she might be baffled, like as not
She'll think you're a resourceful sort of chap,
And count your love a feather in her cap.

CLITON: You seem to know what lying's all about,
But what'll happen if she finds you out?

DORANTE: No problem: by that stage it shouldn't matter,
Since I'll already be *persona grata* -
And after that, if rivals *do* intrude,
My lies can be a sort of amorous code.
That's how it's done.

CLITON: I had no right to scoff -
I've mounted a high horse and fallen off!
Wizards have conjured banquets up from scratch,
So legend tells us, but they're not a patch
On yours! I think you ought to take up writing:
Your books'd sell like hot cakes, what with fighting,

And feasts; and you could make your heroes fly
Around the world in no time – why not try?
You'd make a fortune with a knack like yours –
You could fill tomes with miracles and wars!

DORANTE: When I hear people tell fantastic tales,
I like to take the wind out of their sails
By cooking up some story of my own,
To better theirs, and make them quieten down.
I'm brilliant at it – if you only knew
What a tremendous thrill I get. . . .

CLITON: I do.
But I'm afraid this harmless habit may
Get you into a nasty scrape some day.

DORANTE: We can cross that bridge when we come to it.
This idle chat won't help my cause one bit.
Let's go and find the lady. Follow me –
I'll teach you all about dishonesty!

Exeunt.

ACT TWO

First, above – a room in Clarice's house, in the Place Royale. Thereafter, and for the rest of the play, outside in the square or above in Lucrèce's house, which adjoins Clarice's.

Géronte, Clarice.

CLARICE: I know, Monsieur Géronte, that as your son
He's quite a catch, but how could anyone
Marry a man they've never even met?
I'm not that desperate for a husband . . . yet.
Suppose I did encourage his advances –
Received him as a lover – circumstances
Might change – you might go back on it yourself,
Leaving me compromised – and on the shelf.
I want to see him, but my modesty
Would be in doubt if he was seen with me.

GERONTE: Such beauty and such brains! I can't contest
The justice of so reasoned a request.
Look: I'll be walking, in an hour or so,
Under your window, with Dorante in tow.
I'll find some pretext to detain him there,
So you can judge, from looks, and general air,
The sort of husband that I'm offering you.
He's been at Poitiers for a year or two,
But he's not the scholastic type at all –
Few courtiers are so elegant and tall.
In case you think I'm biased, everyone
Who knows him says so. He's my only son,
And nothing but the very best will do
For him, Clarice – that's why I've chosen *you*.
I'll go and fetch him now. Don't run away.

CLARICE: I wouldn't dream of it, monsieur. Good day.

Exit Géronte.

Enter Lucrèce.

LUCRECE: Good morning. I bumped into old Géronte
As I was coming up – what did he want?

CLARICE: It was about that son of his again –
Dorante.

LUCRECE: *(Laughingly)* "The best, most beautiful of men!"

CLARICE: He's bringing him this morning, if you please,
So I can judge whether his . . . qualities
Are what the old man's cracked them up to be
By spying on him from my balcony!
I must admit, though, I can hardly wait
To see him for myself – I feel my fate
Is almost sealed already, on the strength
Of these reports.

LUCRECE: You'll see him at arm's length.
It's better that way.

CLARICE: Yes; but there again
How can I say I've really judged him, when
I've only had a look at his physique?
What good are looks, when it's the heart we seek?
A fraud can often prosper, undetected,
Thanks to the outward charms that he's perfected.
Although, when marrying, one needs to see to
Choose well, one's heart must have the right of veto.
The task – although essential – of the eyes
Is not to execute, but to advise.
Marriage is like a chain that binds for life –
Compatability of man and wife
Is vital, and it simply wouldn't do
To choose a man I'd never spoken to.

LUCRECE: Speak to him, then.

CLARICE: But there's Alcippe – I can't.

LUCRECE: To Hell with him – you may prefer Dorante!
But if you're worried that he'll hear about
These goings on, I'll try to help you out . . .
I've got no jealous lovers . . . I could write
Dorante a note . . . ask him to come tonight,
To meet me at my window. He, being young
And virile, as we've heard, should go along
With this proposal – but you'll take my place –
It'll be dark, so he won't see your face –
Alcippe'll never know he spoke with you,
And you can find out more about him, too.

CLARICE: Ingenious! And you're sure you wouldn't mind. . . ?

LUCRECE: I'm good at writing letters of that kind!
But what about this morning's interview?
I rather liked our soldier friend. . . .

CLARICE: Me too!
If Dorante has a tenth of that man's charms,
Alcippe be damned – I'll rush into his arms!

LUCRECE: Talk of the Devil – here's the very man.
I'd better go and execute our plan.

Exit.

Enter Alcippe, melodramatically.

ALCIPPE: Clarice! Clarice! You faithless Jezebel!

CLARICE: *(Aside)* Don't say he knows already! How the Hell
Did he find out? *(To Alcippe.)* It's you, Alcippe – hello.
What's wrong?

ALCIPPE: What's wrong! As if you didn't know.
Just ask your conscience – *it* should fill you in.

CLARICE: Sshh! You'll disturb my father with your din.

ALCIPPE: Convenient, your father, isn't he?
Now you can wheel him out to silence me,
And yet he seems to pose few obstacles
To boating trips, and midnight spectacles
"*Sur l'eau*".

CLARICE: "*Sur*" what?

ALCIPPE: That's right, brazen it out.

CLARICE: Brazen what out? What are you on about?

ALCIPPE: You ought to die of shame to hear those words.

CLARICE: Which words? "*Sur l'eau*"? Alcippe, don't be absurd.

ALCIPPE: Perhaps, if I went over the whole story
Of your debauchery in all its gory
Details, you might just blush!

CLARICE: Debauchery!

ALCIPPE: But failing that, Clarice, don't torture me
With mock incomprehension.

CLARICE: You're insane!
Tell me what's wrong – I'm sure I can explain.

ALCIPPE: If I'm insane, it's not with love for you:
I've had a revelation!
(Casts a pious look heavenward.)
I've seen through
That dazzling exterior, to the core –
And found a monster – a rampaging whore!!

CLARICE: You'd better have a decent explanation
For these outrageous claims. . . .

ALCIPPE: My information
Came from the horse's mouth: your lover made
No secret of his conquest, I'm afraid.

CLARICE: Really? And what's his name?

ALCIPPE: Dorante.

CLARICE: Dorante!

ALCIPPE: You can go on pretending if you want.

CLARICE: I've never met him.

ALCIPPE: Oh? Then tell me how
His father came to be with you just now.
You've planned it well – aren't you the clever one?
By day the father . . . and by night the son!

CLARICE: His father's been a friend of ours for years.

ALCIPPE: Oh, reminiscing, were you?! It appears
You have no sense at all of your disgrace.

CLARICE: I haven't even seen this person's face!

ALCIPPE: Too dark, was it? There was no concert, then?
No splendid six course banquet? Tell me, when
Those fireworks suddenly lit up the sky,
Did they distract your gaze? Perhaps that's why
You never saw his face? You mean to say
That when you danced, you looked the other way?!
It seems he really put you off!! Come, come –
You must have seen it when he took you home.
(Pause) I think I've said enough.

CLARICE: More than enough.

ALCIPPE: Oh, that's right, cast me as the ranting, rough,
Irrational lover.

CLARICE: *(Calmer)* Alcippe, somebody's
Been playing games with you.

ALCIPPE: Yes. You have!

CLARICE: Please . . .

ALCIPPE: Give up – it's no use looking for excuses:
I know your devious mind – your little ruses
Are like an open book to me. Goodbye!
Dorante is now the apple of your eye.
I won't make trouble for you – I'll just fade
Away.

CLARICE: Please hear me out. . . .

ALCIPPE: *(With heavy sarcasm.)* But I'm afraid
Your father might come down. . . .

CLARICE: I swear to you –
This accusation simply isn't true.

ALCIPPE: But swearing it proves nothing – I demand
A pledge: the solemn promise of your hand,
Sealed with a kiss.

CLARICE: A kiss?

ALCIPPE: That's right. . . .

CLARICE: I can't!

ALCIPPE: Then it's goodbye – a kiss is what I want.

CLARICE: But I'm afraid my father might come down!

ALCIPPE: You're laughing at me. Am I such a clown?
I'm going.

CLARICE: Go, then. No one's stopping you.

ALCIPPE: I mean it. . . .

CLARICE: So do I.

ALCIPPE: I'm leaving. . . .

CLARICE: DO!

Alcippe leaves the house, emerging in the square below.

ALCIPPE: The more she laughs at me, the less I care:
Love's chains are breaking, ice is forming where
The flames of passion burned before. I feel
A righteous wrath - or is it vengeful zeal? -
Taking control: Dorante must make this good
By trial of arms; if he's a man, he should
Agree to one. The issue's going to be
Clarice's happiness - or misery.
I'll challenge him today - I cannot face
The prospect of a rival in my place.
I'd rather shed my blood, to the last drop,
Than hand her over to that facile fop!
Old friendship's wilting fast, and enmity
Is growing in its place . . . what's this I see?
Dorante! He's with his father . . . I'll withdraw:
It's not yet time to tell him what's in store.

Exit.

Enter Dorante, Géronte and Cliton - Clarice above.

GERONTE: Slow down, Dorante - you're walking me to death!
Let's stop a while - please - let me catch my breath.
(Looks up to check Clarice is there.)
We'll all sit down. Give me a hand, Cliton -
My limbs won't bend these days - I'm getting on.

CLITON: Nonsense, sir - you're as frisky as a lamb.

GERONTE: It pays to be sincere, Cliton.

CLITON: I am.
Now, someone not a million miles away. . . .

DORANTE: Cliton, shut up.

GERONTE: No - let him have his say.
Go on.

CLITON: Well, sir . . .

DORANTE: What an enchanting square!
I think there must be magic in the air:
This morning, for example, I was shown
An island that I'd last seen overgrown
With shrubs and trees, but which is now aglow
With gorgeous edifices - it's as though

Some modern Joshua's trumpet's just been blown,
And walls sprung up, instead of falling down.

GERONTE: Such transformations happen every day
In Paris now: the Left Bank, the Palais
Royal – a splendid capital has leapt
Out of an old ditch, almost while we slept.
It's all so beautiful, you'd be forgiven
For thinking it was built for gods to live in,
Or kings, at least. Let's change the subject, though:
You're everything to me, Dorante. . . .

DORANTE: I know.
And your affection, father, is as dear
To me as life itself.

GERONTE: But the career
That you've embarked on, in your youthful thirst
For glory, will be plunging you head first
Into appalling dangers. Since you are
My only child, before you go to war
I think you should get married: it's my prayer
That once you've got a wife you'll take more care
When marching into battle, and increase
Your chances of survival. . . .

DORANTE: *(Aside)* Blast! Lucrèce!

GERONTE: The bride I have in mind for you is chaste,
Beautiful, rich . . .

DORANTE: But why this sudden haste?

GERONTE: Wait till you've seen the girl: she's quite a catch –
You couldn't hope to make a better match.
For brains and beauty she can have few peers;
Her father's been a friend of mine for years.
My mind's made up.

DORANTE: It makes me ill at ease
To ponder such responsibilities –
I'm far too young.

CLITON: Young men do what they're told.

DORANTE: Stay out of this! *(To Géronte.)* A soldier must be bold
In battle, if he wants to win renown.

GERONTE: Before some death-crazed German hacks you down,
I want an heir – a prop for my old age –
A grandson to preserve my lineage.
And only you can give me one. . . .

DORANTE: I shan't.

GERONTE: What do you mean, you shan't?

DORANTE: I mean I can't.

GERONTE: What do you mean, you can't. Aren't you a man?

DORANTE: I don't mean can't . . . I mean already can. . . .

GERONTE: That's better. . . .

DORANTE: Something happened . . . in Poitiers . . .

GERONTE: Go on.

DORANTE: You're sure. . . ?

GERONTE: Say what you have to say.

DORANTE: I'm married.

CLITON/ GERONTE: WHAT?!!

GERONTE: Without consulting me?

DORANTE: I'm sure you have enough authority
To get the thing annulled. But as things stood
I had no choice . . . I don't believe I could . . .
In fact, I'm sure I couldn't – if you knew. . . .

GERONTE: Don't dither – tell me everything.

DORANTE: Will do.
She's from a noble family – a bit
Penurious perhaps, but. . . .

GERONTE: Out with it!
Her name?

DORANTE: Orphise.

GERONTE: Her father's?

DORANTE: Armédon.

GERONTE: I've never heard of him, but please go on.

DORANTE: Very soon after my arrival there
I met Orphise. Her charms, beyond compare,
Would have subdued a heart of flint. Her gaze
Transfixed me with its bright, soul-searching rays.
I sought an introduction: the reward
For my attentions was her kind regard;
Within six months she had returned my love
With secret favours . . . nothing to reprove
Until at last I had obtained the right
To climb into her bedroom, late at night. . . .
Just for a chat. One night – I can remember
The date – it was the second of November –
(It was the night that I was caught, you see)
Her father had been dining out, and we
Heard him come up the stairs, and stop, and knock
On the bedroom door. Orphise got quite a shock!
She froze, then blenched, then blushed, then used her head –
She drew the curtains round me in the bed,
And let him in. She seemed to have a plan:
She hugged him – almost choked the poor old man –
So that it wouldn't look as though he'd caught her
Off guard. He took a seat, and told his daughter
He'd just received a very handsome offer
For her hand! Picture what I had to suffer.
She managed to respond so cleverly
As to please him, without alarming me.
At length they finished this distressing chat –
But just as he was going out – guess what?
My watch began to strike! He dropped the latch,
And said: "I didn't know you had a watch.
Who gave it you?" "Cousin Acaste," she stalled,
"Just brought it round – he wants it overhauled.
It seems to go off every other minute.
His quarter's got no decent jewellers in it."
"Give it to me. That's easily corrected,"
He said. Orphise came over to collect it –
I passed it through the curtains, but in vain –
My pistol got entangled with the chain,
Which pulled the trigger and discharged a shot.
Disaster! Orphise fainted on the spot.
Her father hurled himself on to the floor,
And shouted "*Assassins!*" and "*Au secours!*"

His son and several servants blocked my path,
But I was practically insane with wrath:
I drew my sword and tried to force my way
Between them, but, in the ensuing fray,
My rapier snapped, which forced me to give ground.
Meanwhile, Orphise was starting to come round:
Recent events had clearly stunned her, but
She was sufficiently alert to shut
The bedroom door, with only her and me
Inside. We both began, spontaneously,
To pile up boxes, tables, chairs and beds,
In a huge barricade; we'd lost our heads –
As if our puny efforts could achieve
Anything better than a brief reprieve!
They smashed a hole and entered through the wall –
I saw the game was up, and had to call
Our struggle to a halt.

GERONTE: I can't infer
From what you've said, you had to marry her!

DORANTE: I'd compromised the girl – what could I do?
Found in her bedroom, and at midnight, too!
I had to marry her to save her honour,
In view of the apparent wrong I'd done her.
What's more, I was outnumbered five to one –
Now tell me, father, what would you have done?
Besides, the ordeal that we'd just been through
Together made me feel her charms anew.
And so, in one fell swoop, I saved my life,
Salvaged a girl's good name and gained a wife.
Now, do your worst.

GERONTE: Calm down, Dorante – I'm not
As heartless as you seem to think: your lot
Deserves some sympathy; but you were wrong
To keep it hidden from me for so long.

DORANTE: I was afraid you'd say she was too poor.

GERONTE: Don't be absurd – what do you take me for?
I care too much about your happiness
To have you marrying under duress –
The girl appears to love you, and it's clear

That you love her – I mustn't interfere.
I'd better go and break it to Clarice.

Exit.

DORANTE: He swallowed it! That was a masterpiece!
A lesser man, in such a situation,
Would have betrayed that fatal hesitation,
And fallen back on tearful pleas, too late
To save him from his matrimonial fate.
It shows you what a damned good lie can do.

CLITON: You mean to say that none of that was true?

DORANTE: Of course not – it was just a brilliant piece
Of fantasy, to save me for Lucrèce.

CLITON: So you made up that stuff about the sword,
The pistol and the watch?

DORANTE: Yes – every word.

CLITON: Sir, I'm your valet, and it's only fair
That you should tip me off, so I can share
These little japes of yours. I have to say,
Though you'd already done it twice today,
I was completely taken in that time.

DORANTE: Never again: as of this moment, I'm
Appointing you my private secretary –
You're going to be the sole repository
Of all my amorous secrets. As for her,
She's half in love with me already. . . .

Enter Sabine.

SABINE: Sir. . . .

DORANTE: *(To Cliton.)* Who's this?

CLITON: I've no idea. Quite pretty, though.
Why not seduce her, since you're in full flow?

DORANTE: *(Sour)* Ha, ha.

SABINE: SIR! Read this letter.

DORANTE: Who's it from?

SABINE: My mistress, sir – Lucrèce.

DORANTE: *(Reading the letter.)* Tell her I'll come.

Exit Sabine.

DORANTE: Well, now there can't be any doubt
About their names: Lucrèce has sought me out.
She wants me there tonight, under her window,
For a romantic chat. Do you still cling to
Your theory that she was the other one –
That oh-so-captivating mute? Come on!

CLITON: It's true, the odds against it have increased –
But wait until your rendez-vous, at least.

DORANTE: Now, off you go – see what you can unearth
About her family . . . and what she's worth.

Exit Cliton.

Enter Lycas.

LYCAS: Monsieur. . . . *(Hands Dorante a letter.)*

DORANTE: Another note – who might you be?

LYCAS: I'm Monsieur Alcippe's valet.

DORANTE: Probably
A supper invitation: *(Reading)* ". . . grave offence . . .
Single combat . . . immediate recompense . . .
Reply at once . . ."!!? Tell him I'm on my way.
(Exit Lycas.)
A challenge! From Alcippe! Well, what a day!
Already I'm engaged to fight a duel . . .
Married . . . in love . . . I think that's pretty cool.
A lawsuit now would make it a grand slam. . . .
(Looks around as though half expecting a third note.)
Quite a début! I've shown how good I am
At getting into awkward spots, but when
It comes to getting out of them again,
I'm in a class apart, as you'll soon see.
Now for this fool who dares to challenge me.

Exit.

END OF ACT TWO

ACT THREE

Place Royale.

Philiste, Dorante, Alcippe.

Dorante and Alcippe have just been fighting, and are out of breath.

PHILISTE: You fought courageously – masculine pride
Has suffered no reverse on either side.
It's lucky I arrived in time to act
As mediator, and enforce a pact
While you were still unharmed. Such chances are
A source of joy, no matter how bizarre.

DORANTE: You find it mystifying? So do I:
I've fought a duel, and I still don't know why!
(To Alcippe.) Perhaps you'd be so kind as to inform me
What has induced this sudden loathing for me?
Has some malicious rumour reached your ears?
Tell me. I'll clear myself, and Philiste here's
My witness.

ALCIPPE: Stop pretending you don't know.

DORANTE: Whatever you've been told, it isn't so.

ALCIPPE: You seem intent on messing me about.
Well then, since you insist, I'll spell it out:
I've loved this girl for years, and she loves me –
At least, she did – but now, apparently,
You've ousted me with music, banquets and
Fireworks, although you clearly understand
The situation – since that's obviously
Why you returned without informing me.
But now you've chosen to come out of hiding:
Secrecy bores you – you prefer deriding
Your beaten rival with a full report
On your romantic exploits. I'd have thought
I had good reason to be shocked and wounded
By such behaviour.

DORANTE: We've already sounded
Each other out in combat – otherwise
I wouldn't bother to refute these lies:

I'd meet you as a rival, man to man.
It's fortunate that, as things stand, I can
Answer these charges without losing face.
The lady who agreed last night to grace
My party with her presence couldn't be
The subject of your jealous fantasy –
She's married, and besides, she's only been
In town a week, you can't have even seen
Her yet.

ALCIPPE: Good lord! You're not my rival, then!

DORANTE: Correct.

ALCIPPE: Come here! *(They embrace.)*
We can be friends again!

DORANTE: Next time Alcippe, think twice before you leap
To desperate conclusions. Try to keep
Things in perspective – exercise restraint.
You seem to have a tendency to paint
Yourself into a corner. Anyhow,
I must be off.

Exit.

ALCIPPE: Damnation!!

PHILISTE: What's wrong now?

ALCIPPE: This only takes me from the frying pan
Into the fire: I haven't traced the man
Who gave that party, and until I do
I'll have no peace.

PHILISTE: Calm down: she still loves you.

ALCIPPE: How do you know?

PHILISTE: To put you at your ease,
The object of last night's festivities
Was someone else. As far as I can gauge
From further detailed questioning, my page
Had got it wrong, or only partly right:
Lucrèce was at Clarice's house last night,
Along with several other friends of hers.
Later he saw two ladies, masked, emerge
And take Lucrèce's carriage, whereupon

He drew the same conclusion we'd have done:
Mistook these girls - Hippolyte and Daphné -
For Clarice and Lucrèce. They made their way
Down to the Seine, my page in hot pursuit -
Heaven knows what possessed the lad to do it -
And there he saw them get into a boat;
He heard "some ghastly music" (that's a quote) -
Saw dinner served - the rest is history -
The carriage had been lent to them, you see -
Having misled himself, he misled us -
There was no need for this appalling fuss.
While they were being entertained and fed,
Clarice was fast asleep, in her own bed.

ALCIPPE: *(Exasperated)* I've shouted at a goddess - that's a sin!
What an absurd predicament I'm in!

PHILISTE: I'll make your peace. But this should give you pause:
Our friend Dorante - the more immediate cause
Of your distress - an expert, as we know,
At instant parties - who, a month ago,
Arrived in Paris secretly, and slips
Outdoors at night, on surreptitious trips
To Madame X's house - spent all last night
Asleep - recovering, as well he might,
After a long day's journey from Poitiers!

ALCIPPE: You mean the banquet. . . ?

PHILISTE: Lies - although he may,
Of course, have dreamed of giving one!

ALCIPPE: Dorante,
Who fought so bravely, and so well? It can't
Be true. A liar? It just doesn't fit -
The school of gallantry would not admit
A scoundrel - the courageous man eschews
Such base and vicious pranks - in fact, he'd choose
Death before falsehood. No. It's rubbish.

PHILISTE: Why? A
Man can be brave by nature, but a liar
By force of habit. Far from being fazed
By this discovery, you should be amazed
At our credulity: a feast, a ball,
Four orchestras, thousands of fireworks - all

Produced from nowhere in an hour or two –
A sort of party *ex machina* – who
But a rank cretin would have swallowed it?
I had my doubts – his story didn't fit
With what I'd heard – but you. . . ?

ALCIPPE: My jealousy,
As can so often happen, blinded me.
I believed what I feared. But let's dismiss
Dorante's absurdities, and find Clarice.
Help me to beg forgiveness. Now I see
Why she refused to blush!

PHILISTE: Leave it to me.
Wait till tomorrow – a full explanation
From me should help to ease the situation.
You mustn't try to swim against the tide –
Leave time for her resentment to subside.

ALCIPPE: As usual, there's a lot in what you say,
But look! It's her! She's bound to come this way.
I'll take your tip – avoid her now and bide
My time until she's seen the funny side.

Exeunt.

Enter Clarice and Lucrèce.

CLARICE: I can't get over it! To think that he
And my admirer from the Tuileries
Are the same person!

LUCRECE: *And* a lying rogue!
Not that that matters: lying is in vogue –
Young scholars are inventing ever more
Adventurous disguises, and the war
Is very fertile ground – they're constantly
Boasting about their 'feats' in Germany
To any girl who's gullible enough
To listen – and to prove they know their stuff,
They spout a catalogue of past campaigns,
Complete with itemised losses and gains,
Conned from the last gazette. Some cavaliers
Have scarcely ventured out of town in years,
Probably only doing so to visit
Their families. But they do have exquisite

Imaginations, which is half the battle
When dishing up such mock-heroic prattle.
Our friend has told himself he won't impress
A woman of your calibre, unless
He can convince her he's the type of man
Whose plume is in his hat, not in his hand –
And hence this veteran act of his – he's trying
To storm his way into your life by lying.

CLARICE: He's certainly a master of the art –
Apparently he's broken Alcippe's heart
With no less dazzling a fantasy
About a party that he gave for me
Last night. This piece of blatant fabrication
Has led to some outrageous accusations
On Alcippe's part, with talk of music, dancing,
A six-course banquet, with a quite entrancing
Array of dishes – anyone who had
A meal like that would have to be quite mad!

LUCRECE: This shows how deep in love Dorante must be –
Passion enhances ingenuity.
He must have known Alcippe was courting you –
That's what this string of lies was meant to do –
Frighten him off. And now the coast is clear,
He wastes no time, but sends his father here
To speak to yours. He got here yesterday,
And he's as good as married you! I'd say
He's ten times more resourceful than Alcippe –
In fact, he makes him look an utter drip.
Your fathers have agreed. You want him. He
Clearly wants you. It's a *fait accompli*.

CLARICE: Don't speak too soon.

LUCRECE: You can't have changed your mind. . . .

CLARICE: If you're so certain, see if you can find
Some explanation for his blackguardry –
Or maybe you approve of bigamy.

LUCRECE: What?!

CLARICE: Yes – he's married, and his father came
To call the whole thing off – covered in shame
He was, to do him justice.

LUCRECE: It's my turn
To call Dorante a rogue! You live and learn!
He lies to everybody, willy-nilly –
Who ever heard of anything so silly?!
Why did he bother spouting all that tosh –
Surely he must have known it wouldn't wash?
But you're still meeting him – why, may I ask?
To laugh at him, or to take him to task?

CLARICE: To have the pleasure of exposing him –
Allow me to indulge a foolish whim.

LUCRECE: I'd rather make him wait all night out here.

CLARICE: Sshh! That's him now – we'd better disappear!
Your balcony is the appointed place –
If I stay here I'll meet him face to face.
Alcippe will do for me – his jealous rage
Ought to be fairly easy to assuage,
Now that we know Dorante a little better.

They go into Lucrèce's house.

Enter Dorante and Cliton.

DORANTE: This is the time she gave me in the letter.

CLITON: I found out quite a lot about her, sir:
Her father's rich, and has no child but her –
An advocate – comes from a very old
French family – the girl's of age, I'm told.
(Hands Dorante notes.)
It'd be really something, in my view,
If she was brilliant at lying, too:
I'd love to see her beat you at your own
Outrageous game.

DORANTE: The world has rarely known
Talent like mine – one needs a combination
Of timing, memory, imagination,
Wit, daring, fluency . . . what have we here?
She's opening her window – let's draw near.

Clarice and Lucrèce are now above, in Lucrèce's chamber, Dorante and Cliton in the square below.

LUCRECE: Good luck, Clarice, you're speaking for me now –
You'll humble him as only you know how.

He's certainly deserved it – all the same,
I'm half regretting lending you my name.
It's possible, in different circumstances,
That I myself might welcome his advances.

CLARICE: If pigs could fly, or if the moon was blue,
I might consider welcoming them too.

LUCRECE: I'll stay and listen in, if that's alright.

CLARICE: Where is he? Can you see him in this light?

LUCRECE: He's got his valet with him – look, down there.

DORANTE: *(Calling up.)* I'm here, madame, and ready to declare
In life, in death, allegiance to your throne.

LUCRECE: It doesn't sound as though he's changed his tone.

CLARICE: Such impudence! Do you suppose he might
Have recognised my voice?

CLITON: *(In a whisper to Dorante.)* Sir, you were right
About their names – that's certainly the one
Who talked so much this morning.

DORANTE: Hush, Cliton!
This heinous fault, Lucrèce, I can't undo:
I've wasted decades not adoring you!
I can't imagine a more gruesome plight
Than spending half an hour out of your sight!
In fact, it's been a sort of living death –
Loving you's tantamount to drawing breath!

CLARICE: *(To Lucrèce.)* First me, now you – who's next?

LUCRECE: *(To Clarice.)* God only knows.
Fictitious love needs practice, I suppose.

DORANTE: Nature equipped me for a single cause:
To lose my life in the defence of yours!
Do with me what you will – just tell me, now,
When you intend to use your slave, and how.

CLARICE: I had a little something to suggest,
But as things stand, I think it might be best
If we forgot it.

DORANTE: Tell me where to go –

What friend to kill, what king to overthrow!
I'll do it now . . .

CLARICE: But would you marry me?

DORANTE: At once.

CLARICE: And go to jail for bigamy?

DORANTE: Bigamy?! *(Pause)* Somebody's been telling lies.

CLITON: *(Aside)* You don't say!

LUCRECE: *(To Clarice)* Fancy that!

CLARICE: *(To Lucrèce.)* WHAT a surprise!

DORANTE: If this is just your way of testing me. . . .

CLARICE: Give up. You've lost all credibility.

DORANTE: But you're the only woman in my life.
May lightning strike me if I've got a wife!

CLARICE: Swear if you like – liars are always free
With oaths.

DORANTE: Perhaps you never cared for me.
But if you did, and if these false reports
Are all that's making you have second thoughts,
Then you've no reason to reject my love:
Such slanders I can easily disprove.

CLARICE: *(To Lucrèce.)* You must admit, it's a convincing act –

LUCRECE: *(To Clarice.)* Rarely did fiction sound so much like fact.

DORANTE: *(Kneeling)* To make it clear exactly how things stand,
I'm on my knees and asking for your hand.
Please – say you'll marry me – tomorrow. . . .

CLARICE: *When?*
You might have married fifty girls by then!

DORANTE: You're quite a catch, you know – the man who carries
You off will make some enemies in Paris.

CLARICE: I'm tempted to accept you – you deserve
A lot of enemies. You have the nerve
To call yourself a soldier! Were you made
A corporal in the Pen and Ink brigade?
You came to court a year ago, you say –

I didn't know the court was at Poitiers!
And don't you think it's just a little steep
To claim you gave a party in your sleep?
To conjure wives out of the air, and then
Abruptly make them disappear again?
How can one feel respect for such a man?

CLITON: *(In a whisper to Dorante.)*
Oh dear! Get out of this one if you can.

DORANTE: Watch me. *(To Clarice.)*
Some day, when we've more leisure, I
Can furnish you with reasons for each lie.
For the time being, though, let's concentrate
On what concerns us most: why fabricate
That marriage? Yes – it *was* a fabrication,
But one that should inspire your admiration –
Far from discrediting me, it'll prove
What lengths I'm going to to keep your love.

CLARICE: *Keep* it indeed!

DORANTE: Just listen. . . .

CLITON: Wait a minute –
If it's a lie you're telling, don't begin it
Without me knowing.

DORANTE: *(To Cliton.)* I could always tear
Your tongue out, I suppose!
(To Clarice). Lucrèce, I care
For nobody but you, so when my father
Told me he planned a marriage for me, rather
Than fall into another woman's clutches. . . .

CLARICE: *(To Lucrèce.)* He's off again.

DORANTE: . . . . I feigned a marriage. Such is
My skill at lying that the old man swallowed
The story, and forgiveness quickly followed.
It's natural for a lady to object
To such dishonesty, but please reflect
On what inspired it – on my love for you,
In other words – and try to love me, too.
The only match I really want to make
Is one with you – all others, real or fake,

I shun, and welcome now, with open arms,
The tyranny of your all-conquering charms!

CLARICE: Monsieur, it isn't good for one, you know,
To fan the flames of nascent passion so.
More to the point, though, how can I be sure
My 'charms' have such a powerful allure
For you? You've only met me once; you know
Nothing at all about me . . .

DORANTE: Don't I, though?!
(He consults Cliton's notes.)
Your mother's dead. Your father's a first-rate
And fabulously wealthy advocate –
One Periandre – whose fees are sure to clear
A staggering two thousand crowns this year.
Your brother died, fighting in Italy –
You also had a sister called . . . *(Squinting at the notes.)* Julie.
As far as I can gather she's dead, too.

CLARICE: That's *you*, Lucrèce. He *is* in love with you.

LUCRECE: *(With a sigh.)* I wonder!

CLARICE: *(To Lucrèce.)* What's his game? We'll soon find out.
(To Dorante.)
There's something else we need to talk about,
And that's Clarice; it *was* six hours ago,
But weren't you rather taken with her?

DORANTE: No.
You shouldn't need to test me in this way –
I've done enough to prove my love today.
Haven't I bared my soul? Haven't I shown
That I belong to you, and you alone?
As for Clarice – she's neither here nor there –
She might as well be dead, for all I care.

CLARICE: You must be very difficult to please –
Clarice's father's wealthy too, and she's. . . .
Not unattractive. You consider me
More beautiful, but I can tell you, she
Won't have to look for eligible men.

DORANTE: Indeed? I'm very happy for her, then.
She's not my type, however; I'd prefer
An Ethiope or an English girl to her!

CLARICE: But that's impossible – I heard you say
How much you were in love with her, today!

DORANTE: You've been deceived again.

CLARICE: *(To Lucrèce.)* Wait for the oath.

DORANTE: I swear to God. . . .

CLARICE: *(To Lucrèce.)* Told you.

DORANTE: I've met you both,
But you're the only girl I've spoken to
Today.

CLARICE: I'd give this up if I were you.
It's quite absurd – expecting me to fall
For that, when I was there, and heard it all.
It's too ridiculous! Please go away.
I've had enough amusement for one day.

Closes window.

CLITON: She's found you out – what are you going to do?

DORANTE: The meeting wasn't a success, it's true.

CLITON: It couldn't've gone worse. But don't despair. . . .
Perhaps it was my fault for being there. . . .
(Clapping his hands in ironic realisation.)
You must've used that secret code of yours –
The one for fooling gooseberries – of course!
She loves you, then, and I'm the gooseberry fool!
There's just no keeping up with you – it's cruel!

DORANTE: Very funny. I take it you'd advise
Abandoning this amorous enterprise?

CLITON: If it was mine, I'd sell it on the spot.

DORANTE: Love's priceless.

CLITON: Yours is definitely not.
I'd give . . . two sous for it – possibly three.

DORANTE: How could she doubt my love for her?

CLITON: *(Heavy irony.)* Search me.
Though you do have a tendency to lie
To everyone you meet – perhaps that's why.

DORANTE: But everything I said just now was true!

CLITON: It was?

DORANTE: You know it was. . . .

CLITON: Perhaps I do. . . .
The only trouble is, when liars tell
The truth, it tends to have a fishy smell.

DORANTE: Maybe, if some third party put my case,
She'd listen to it with a better grace.
Women are whimsical – I wouldn't be
At all surprised if she was testing me.
Before I go to bed I'll try and find
Some strategy to make her change her mind.
It shouldn't be too hard to put things right –
Some of my best ideas I have at night!

Exeunt.

END OF ACT THREE

ACT FOUR

The Place Royale, early next morning.

Dorante, Cliton.

CLITON: You know what hours fashionable ladies keep –
Lucrèce is bound to want her beauty sleep.

DORANTE: The early bird catches the worm. Besides,
Lucrèce's house is where my heart resides.

CLITON: Well, it'll need one of your smartest tricks
To get you out of this particular fix.

DORANTE: Well, now – as I lay pining in the dark
I happened to remember your remark
About the wondrous influence of largesse –
You claimed it was the secret of success
In love.

CLITON: I said it worked on a coquette –
Not on the sort of girl you're trying to get.

DORANTE: Of course. I know Lucrèce – she's too refined,
Too good, to let a present change her mind.
Her servants, on the other hand, might well
Succumb to bribes – I'm sure she'd give them Hell
If she found out about it – nonetheless,
A few of them are bound to acquiesce.
I'd pay a lot for any information
That helped to clarify the situation.
We've got to find that maid. . . .

CLITON: You're right: take me –
I'm always giving in to bribery.
A friendly deed deserves some gratitude,
And bribes are friendly – that's my attitude.

DORANTE: *(Amused)* Let's hope the girl's as principled as you.

CLITON: We'll soon find out, sir, but before we do
You ought to know, I've heard a strange report
About Alcippe – apparently he's fought
A duel!

DORANTE: *(Mock surprise.)* He has?! When was this?

CLITON: Yesterday,
It seems.

DORANTE: With whom?

CLITON: My sources didn't say –
Although they did describe a person who,
I must admit, sounded a bit like you.
And if I hadn't been with you all day
I'd have believed it was.

DORANTE: Believe away.
I sent you to Lucrèce's house. . . .

CLITON: That's right!
You mean, you packed me off so you could fight?

DORANTE: He made me promise not to tell a soul,
But you should know about it, in your role
Of . . . what was it?

CLITON: Your private secretary,
And . . .

DORANTE: Yes, of course – the sole repository
Of all my amorous secrets. Very well –
I'll tell you everything there is to tell.
It all began a year ago – Alcippe
Was down in Poitiers on a business trip;
He paid a call on me, and we fell out –
You mustn't ask me what it was about –
We would have fought, but for the intervention
Of friends, and it was always our intention
To settle our dispute the manly way
When next we met, and that was yesterday.
Under your very nose, as we embraced
He whispered in my ear a time and place;
The rest was simple – I dispensed with you,
And hurried to the deadly rendez-vous.
It was a rather off-the-cuff affair –
No seconds – but I beat him fair and square:
Three times I skewered him, like so much meat –
He fell, a bloody bundle, at my feet.
That's how I left him.

CLITON: What?! You mean he's dead?

DORANTE: His case was critical, I would have said.

CLITON: Hang on, though – isn't *that* him over there –
Running towards us now across the square?

Enter Alcippe.

ALCIPPE: *(Breathless)* Dorante! My father!

DORANTE: Eh?!

ALCIPPE: He's just arrived.

CLITON: Either I'm dreaming, or this man's alive!

DORANTE: As for my father, if I had the choice,
I'd never see him, let alone rejoice
At his return.

ALCIPPE: Of course – I should explain
Why I'm so glad to have him here again:
(Poetic) To link Clarice's destiny to mine. . . .
(Prosaic) There were some papers that he had to sign.

DORANTE: I understand. But oughtn't you to go
And tell Clarice?

ALCIPPE: I had to let you know –
After all, you're my oldest friend.

DORANTE: *(Unimpressed)* How sweet!
Now nothing's stopping you – your joy's complete.

ALCIPPE: Right – off I go. I'll see you later, then.
This morning I'm the happiest of men!

Exit.

CLITON: I'm lost for words, sir – getting killed by you
Seems to work wonders – won't you kill me, too?!
What's this in aid of? I'm your secretary –
Not to mention "the sole repository
Of all your amorous secrets". Wasn't I
Meant to be told when you were going to lie?

DORANTE: What makes you think my story wasn't true?

CLITON: I'd swallow any story, sir, for you –
The only trouble is, I think I'd choke:
You tell so many! It's beyond a joke.

Nobody's safe – Turk, Christian and Jew,
Dog, cat and mouse – they've all been conned by you.

DORANTE: You're baffled by Alcippe's recovery –
It seems extremely rapid, I agree.
But medicine has come on by leaps and bounds
In recent years – some of the cures they've found
Are simply staggering: one remedy,
Known to the troops as "powdered sympathy",
Reputedly works wonders in the field.

CLITON: I can believe some nasty wounds have healed.
But resurrection! That's another matter.
You pierced him like a pilchard on a platter,
Or so you said – and now just look at him:
I've never seen a man so full of vim.

DORANTE: But if you give this medicine to dead men,
Before you know it they're alive again.

CLITON: *(Heavy sarcasm.)* Well, fancy that! Give us the recipe,
And you can have my services for free!

DORANTE: I would, but it's in Hebrew, and I doubt
If that's a language you know much about.

CLITON: So you're a Hebrew scholar now? Since when?

DORANTE: I'm good at languages – fluent in ten.

CLITON: But after all, that's hardly a surprise:
One language wouldn't do for all your lies.

DORANTE: You're just an ignoramus – never mind,
Here comes my father.

Enter Géronte.

GERONTE: *(Out of breath.)* Phew! You're hard to find.

DORANTE: *(Aside)* For him, perhaps! A father tends to be a
Burden to the aspiring cavalier.

GERONTE: As I've already said, I see no point
In trying to part a couple God has joined,
In view of which, Dorante, I want to see
This country wife of yours immediately.
I've written to her father, to express
My joy at forming links with the *noblesse*

D'épée, and my impatience to behold
The girl whose myriad virtues you've extolled.
(The sort of gibberish, in other words,
With which one humours twopenny-halfpenny lords.)
I've told him that an old man's hopes depend
On her. What's more, I wouldn't like to send
A mere retainer to collect the girl –
You ought to go, or I'll be thought a churl.

DORANTE: You'll overwhelm him with your courtesy!
Not that I mind – it's all the same to me.
But what's the point? He'd never let her make
So long a journey . . . for the baby's sake.

GERONTE: WHO'S SAKE?!

DORANTE: She's pregnant, father – six months gone.

GERONTE: Six months! *(A tense pause.)* Come here!

Dorante moves uncertainly towards him, and is promptly caught up in a tremulous hug.

I'm overwhelmed! Well done!

DORANTE: So you won't jeopardise the pregnancy?

GERONTE: Of course not – this means far too much to me:
My prayers have all been answered – I must learn
To exercise some patience in return.
But what amazing news! My darling boy!

CLITON: *(Aside)* If he goes on like this he'll die of joy.

GERONTE: I'd best be off. I'll write a different letter –
She mustn't strain herself – in fact, she'd better
Go straight to bed. I'll tell him so. She may be
His daughter, but she's carrying our baby.

Dorante gives way to laughter, but breaks off abruptly as Géronte returns.

You'd better write as well.

DORANTE: I won't forget.
(To Cliton.) He's mad!

CLITON: He isn't out of earshot yet.

GERONTE: *(Re-entering)* What was his name again?

DORANTE: *(Pause, as he tries to recall it.)* Just call him "Sir".
I'll send yours off with mine.

GERONTE: No. I'd prefer
To have his name on it, and in my hand.

DORANTE: He's such a pest!
(To Géronte.) I don't quite understand. . . .

GERONTE: I know these country squires – they're apt to set
Tremendous store by points of etiquette.

DORANTE: Not this one, though, he's spent some time at court . . .

GERONTE: That's immaterial.

DORANTE: I would have thought. . . .

GERONTE: Just give it to me, please.

DORANTE: *(In a whisper to Cliton.)* What *was* his name?

CLITON: *(Aside to Dorante.)* Search me.

DORANTE: His name's . . . Acaste.

GERONTE: That's not the same
As what you told me yesterday. Hang on. . . .
I've got it . . . Armadillo . . . Armédon,
That's it.

DORANTE: Why, yes . . . of course . . . but he's got two.

GERONTE: He has?

DORANTE: *(To Cliton.)* Explain, Cliton.

CLITON: *(To Dorante.)* No. Why don't you?

DORANTE: It's my fault, I suppose . . . I should have told you. . . .
Armédon was his nickname as a soldier,
But he got so attached to it that he. . . .
Uses them both now, interchangeably.

GERONTE: I see. It's not unusual these days
For people to employ such soubriquets.
I'll see you later.

Exit.

DORANTE: That was a close shave.

CLITON: You said yourself, sir, liars need to have
Good memories.

DORANTE: Not always. In this case
Improvisation's taken memory's place.

CLITON: Perhaps, but now the cat's out of the bag.
You're in for trouble – tongues are bound to wag.

DORANTE: You're right, Cliton – time isn't on my side –
The sooner the proverbial knot gets tied
The better. Here's that maid of hers, on cue.

Enter Sabine.

Come here, my girl, I want a word with you.
Yesterday, when you brought that note for me,
I should have tipped you, but my ecstasy
Made me forgetful – it was very rude:
Accept this token of my gratitude.

Offers her a purse.

SABINE: *(With exaggerated coyness.)*
Thanks . . . but I can't.

DORANTE: Take it.

SABINE: You've got me wrong,
If you expect. . . .

DORANTE: Here's more.

He puts more coins into the purse.

Now, come along.
You must accept it – it's a point of honour.
Hold out your hand.

SABINE: No.

CLITON: *(Aside)* What a primadonna!
She needs to learn a bit of *savoir-faire.*
(To Sabine.) Acting like this won't get you anywhere.
It's touching, but in times as hard as these
Servants should pounce on all gratuities:
Hold out your hand, and if one hand won't do,
Just thank your lucky stars and hold out two.
Who needs umbrellas when it's raining gold?
Masters are mean and servants must be bold –

I'm sick of eating humble pie – walk tall!
We could go halves, if you don't want it all.

SABINE: What cheek! Thank you, monsieur – it's kind of you.

She grabs the purse.

DORANTE: There's more, but first there's something you can do
For me: since you're Lucrèce's postman, I
Would like you to deliver my reply –
And here it is. *(Hands her a note.)*

SABINE: I'll give it to her, sir,
But don't you count on it persuading her –
I'll do my best.

CLITON: *(Aside to Dorante.)* Her scruples are retreating.
She's taken my advice and now she's eating
Out of your hand.

DORANTE: *(To Cliton.)* Thank God for bribery!
(To Sabine.) Give her the letter, and report to me
In an hour's time. *(To Cliton.)* I'm off to raise more funds!

SABINE: *(Aside)* Good boy!
(To Dorante.) I'll let you know how she responds.

Exit Dorante.

CLITON: You see? The man's an endless source of money.
I've brought you to the land of milk and honey.

SABINE: It's raining gold, all right – but who needs you?

CLITON: I was the one who told you what to do.

SABINE: I'm not the simpleton you take me for:
The more I seemed to hesitate, the more
He had to give – if that's stupidity,
Then who needs cunning? This'll do for me. *(Jingling the purse.)*

CLITON: If you're so wise, what are my master's chances?
Will she go on rejecting his advances?
Just what exactly is she playing at?

SABINE: I'd like to help a generous man like that –
I'll tell you this – she hardly slept a wink
Last night – she's half in love with him, I think.

CLITON: Really? It must've been the other half
That brought him here last night to have a laugh
At his expense. My master hates half measures –
He much prefers whole women, and whole pleasures.
I've rarely seen a more peculiar species
Of love than this . . . this 'half' love of Lucrèce's.

SABINE: He only needs to give it time, you'll see –
She'll fall in love with him . . . whole-heartedly.

CLITON: That's not how I'd assess the state of play.

SABINE: The trouble is, she doesn't know which way
To turn: she loves him, or at least she's trying,
But how can she be certain he's not lying?
For instance, when they met him yesterday,
He didn't have an honest word to say,
With all that talk of war and gallantry.
It seems he's done it now on two or three
Occasions.

CLITON: Liars do exhaust their range,
And try a bit of truth, just for a change.

SABINE: That may be so, but you can understand
Why she's not sure he really wants her hand.

CLITON: She ought to make her feelings plainer, though –
He had a sleepless night as well, you know.

SABINE: I'll take your word for it.

CLITON: *(With mock solemnity.)* Are you implying
That I, a man of honour, might be lying?

SABINE: He's given up Clarice? You're sure of that?

CLITON: If he's in love with her I'll eat my hat.

SABINE: You swear?

CLITON: I swear.

SABINE: Well, this'll reassure him:
This morning she was on the look-out for him.
She sent me out with orders to discover
If he was still behaving like a lover.
So if he really wants her, as you say,
There's not a great deal standing in his way.

CLITON: Well, what now?

SABINE: You can vanish, for a start –
I shan't need any prompting for this part.

CLITON: All right. Just make her drop her foolish pride,
And I'll take care of the financial side.

Sabine watches him, shaking her head at the arrogance of men.

SABINE: I reckon it's all over, bar the shouting.
Here comes Lucrèce. She must be mad about him.

Enter Lucrèce, out of breath, having hurried from her house as soon as she saw Cliton leave.

LUCRECE: Any news?

SABINE: He's in love with you, all right.

LUCRECE: You're sure?

SABINE: I've got it here, in black and white.

Lucrèce snatches Dorante's letter from her.

LUCRECE: *(Reading the letter.)*
It's pretty passionate, I must admit. . . .
But I still don't believe a word of it.
What good's a declaration and a vow?

SABINE: He's put his money where his mouth is now.

She shows her the purse.

LUCRECE: Sabine! He gave you this?!

SABINE: Don't hit the roof.

LUCRECE: *(Horrified)*
You took a bribe?!

SABINE: I thought you'd want some proof:
A man who bribes a lady's servant must
Be serious.

LUCRECE: Perhaps. Sabine, I trust
You'll keep these windfalls to yourself in future.

SABINE: You should reply to such a generous suitor.

LUCRECE: Tell him I didn't even read his letter. . . .
Tell him I tore it up.

SABINE: *(Aside)* Perhaps I'd better
Forget my dreams of wealth.

LUCRECE: But do take care
Not to plunge him into complete despair –
You could throw in some trite philosophy
About the laws of femininity –
Tell him a woman's anger soon dies down. . . .
And let him know my favourite haunts in town,
So he's a chance of bumping into me.
I'm only testing his resolve, you see.

SABINE: But there's no need to: if you only knew
The sort of agonies that man's been through –
Tossing and turning – brooding all night long. . . .

LUCRECE: Poor thing! I hope he doesn't read me wrong.
He's certainly the man I want, and yet
One has to play a little hard to get.

Enter Clarice.

CLARICE: It seems he really does love you – I've lost
This contest – but at very little cost:
Alcippe makes up for it – his father's here.

LUCRECE: *(Embracing her.)* Oh, darling!

CLARICE: I no longer live in fear
Of endless spinsterhood! But are you sure
Dorante's peculiar passion will endure?
Sabine might take his fancy next! Who knows?

LUCRECE: He's not as volatile as you suppose –
I'm confident of that.

CLARICE: It may be so.
He *might* be capable of love – although
"Might" 's very much the operative word.

LUCRECE: The games he played with us were quite absurd –
But if he keeps this up, perhaps I'll start
To think he may be speaking from the heart.

CLARICE: If you're in love with him, be on your guard –
Always make sure you hold the winning card:

I've never met such a conceited fop –
He's practically on fire with *amour propre.*

LUCRECE: You go too fast: I haven't said that I'm
In love with him – only that, given time,
I might begin to take him at his word.

CLARICE: But that distinction frequently gets blurred:
Once you're convinced of his sincerity,
Vanity being what it is, you'll see
A lot more in him than you did before,
And soon you'll be in love – it's Nature's law.

LUCRECE: And if I told you that he'd written me
A letter, and I'd read it eagerly. . . ?

CLARICE: *(Heavy irony.)* I'd hesitate, but if push came to shove
I'd take that as a further sign of love.

LUCRECE: Or curiosity, since that and passion
Tend to affect us in a similar fashion.

CLARICE: If you say so.

SABINE: Stop it, the pair of you!
What earthly good can you expect to do,
Just standing, bickering the time away?

CLARICE/
LUCRECE: She's right!

LUCRECE: But when we met him yesterday
Aux Tuileries, and he was such a bore
About his so-called "exploits" in the war
You seemed quite taken with him – could it be
That you were merely . . . curious, like me?

CLARICE: Yes, I was curious, but the more he spoke
The more I took his flattery for a joke.

LUCRECE: Why, then you treated *that* the way I've done
His letter – as a piece of harmless fun.

CLARICE: To listen is good manners, as you know –
One's not obliged to read a letter, though.

LUCRECE: Sabine's about to tell him that I tore
His letter up.

CLARICE: *(Teasing again.)* Is she, indeed? What for?
I wouldn't call *that* curiosity –
More like a piece of amorous strategy. . . .

LUCRECE: It's nearly time for mass – we'd better go.
(To Sabine.) And if you come across Dorante . . .

SABINE: I know.
You can rely on me – love's a disease
And I've got lots of sure-fire remedies.

Exeunt Clarice and Lucrèce.

Meanwhile I'll put away this golden rain
Until the skies begin to cloud again.

Gives the purse a final, triumphant shake and exit, other side of stage from the ladies.

END OF ACT FOUR

ACT FIVE

Place Royale.

Géronte, Argante.

GERONTE: This lawsuit's been a millstone round your neck,
Argante.

ARGANTE: I'm just a n-n-nervous wreck.

GERONTE: You should have said: as an old friend of yours
I'd have been happy to promote your cause –
A word or two in the appropriate ear –
I've got a lot of influence up here.
You could have put your feet up in Poitiers
And left it all to me. Oh, by the way,
Speaking of Poitiers, I've been meaning to
Ask you about Acaste.

ARGANTE: A-c-c-who?

GERONTE: Acaste's his given name – not everyone
Knows him as that – some call him Armédon.

ARGANTE: I'm sorry, but I d-d-don't recall
Anyone going by those names at all.

GERONTE: Are you quite sure? My sources tell me he
Comes from a very ancient family.
He held some army post, but he's retired –
While his estate leaves much to be desired,
He has a lovely daughter called Orphise –
You must have heard of *her* – I gather she's
The toast of Poitiers.

ARGANTE: Very possibly.
But if she is it's n-n-news to me.

GERONTE: I know: you're sheltering the boy – that's it!
You needn't bother, though – I'm not a bit
Upset about this marriage of Dorante's:
He's given me what every father wants –
You're looking at a grandfather-to-be;
Perhaps you've heard about the pregnancy?
He's told me everything: how he became

Her husband, as they say, "in all but name",
And then in name, too, after he was found
In bed with her! She hid him, but the sound
First of his watch, and after that his gun,
Gave him away and rather spoiled the fun.
But I've forgiven him, so I repeat:
There's no necessity to be discreet.

ARGANTE: That's utter rubbish, and whoever said it
Must have been t-t-trying to discredit
D-d-dorante – it's inde-ffffensible –
I know your son – he's far too sssssensible
To get himself in such a m-m-mess!

GERONTE: I was amazed myself, I must confess,
But since it came from him it must be true –
I don't see why he'd make it up – do you?
(Suspicious.) What sort of reputation did my son
Have in Poitiers?

ARGANTE: Admired by everyone
For b-b-boldness, f-f-flair and wit –
However, one thing worried us a bit. . . .
He lllll . . . he lllll . . . *(Stamps his foot.)*
– he rarely spoke the truth.

GERONTE: Rarely?

ARGANTE: Not once. It's just a quirk of youth.
With such a wise f-father for a guide
I'm sure he'll put these silly tricks aside.
But d-d-doesn't time f-f-f-fly.
I'm d-d-due in c-c-court. Goodbye!

Exit.

GERONTE: Well? Who's to blame – the father or the son?
Dorante's a liar – I'm a simpleton!
He tells his lies to such superb effect
That each is both direct and indirect –
He lies to further his pernicious ends
And I pass on his nonsense to my friends!

Enter Dorante and Cliton.

Are you a gentleman?

DORANTE: *(Aside)* He's off again.
(To Géronte.)
Sir, I'm your son. Aren't we both gentlemen?

GERONTE: You think that it's enough to share a name?

DORANTE: Ask anyone in France – they'll say the same.

GERONTE: And anyone in France is bound to know
That reputations such as mine don't grow
On trees. What's more, the status we inherit
Is the result of centuries of merit.

DORANTE: Nice of one's ancestors to win renown,
And then so generously hand it down.

GERONTE: But sometimes what our ancestors obtain
Is prodigally thrown away again
By their descendants: for example, you –
You're a descendant – and a scoundrel, too.

DORANTE: Who? Me?!

GERONTE: Yes, you: the work of centuries
Has been destroyed by your outrageous lies.
You were marked down for an exalted place
In French society, but chose disgrace.
To lie as you do, and still claim to be
A gentleman is gross hypocrisy.
If somebody had given him the lie,
A gentleman would be prepared to die
To vindicate his honour, but not you:
Your calmness shows that what I've said is true.

DORANTE: You've got no proof of this.

GERONTE: Have you no shame?
How about this for proof: what's your wife's name?
(Pause, as Dorante tries to remember it.)
I'm waiting . . . and be sure to get it right.

CLITON: *(To Dorante.)*
Don't say it slipped your mind during the night!

GERONTE: Tell me about her father's family.
What were *his* names again? Does he have three?

CLITON: *(To Dorante.)* Can't you remember?

DORANTE: *(To Cliton.)* No!

CLITON: *(To Dorante.)* Then improvise.

GERONTE: I can't believe I swallowed all those lies!
But pretty soon you'll get your just deserts –
It's my stupidity that really hurts.
To let myself be made the tool and toy
Of a mere fop – a callow, impish boy!
Have I offended you? I don't recall
Doing you any serious harm at all.
I've always been as lenient as I could –
I spanked you sometimes, but it did you good.
If you were so revolted by Clarice
You should have said – why fool about like this?
I only wanted you to be content –
I proved it, too, by giving my consent
To your marrying a girl I'd never seen.
And yet, what use has all this kindness been,
If insults and deceit are your idea
Of gratitude? And now, get out of here –
I wash my hands of you.

DORANTE: Please listen.

GERONTE: Why?
You're only going to tell another lie.

DORANTE: The truth this time, and nothing but the truth.

GERONTE: You'd better borrow someone else's mouth.

DORANTE: Yesterday morning, in the Tuileries,
I found a jewel – a woman whom to see
Is to adore, and I can have no peace
Until I've married her. Her name's Lucrèce.

GERONTE: Lucrèce? Where does she live?

DORANTE: Just over there
That pink and yellow house across the square.

GERONTE: Oh, if it's *that* Lucrèce I know her well –
Her father's an old friend, so mind you tell
The truth this time.

DORANTE: Having been instantly
Enslaved by her, picture my agony

When, that same day, you told me that you planned,
To make an offer for Clarice's hand.
I didn't dare disclose my love, in case
Lucrèce's only dowry were her face,
So I pretended I was spoken for.
Was that a crime? All's fair in love and war.
You seemed so adamant - what could I do?
You left me no choice but to lie to you.
But since she has both wealth and pedigree,
I now appeal to you for clemency:
If you'll arrange things with her father, I
Can vouch for her.

GERONTE: I'm sure this is a lie.

DORANTE: Just ask Cliton, if you're in any doubt:
He's been my faithful confidant throughout.

GERONTE: Has he indeed? It seems to me things must
Be pretty bad, if I'm supposed to trust
Your valet more than you! Listen, Dorante:
I like to think I'm fairly tolerant -
I like you - I'm your father, after all -
You've stretched my patience, but I'm going to call
A truce - I'll give you one more chance, although
I hear the voice of reason screaming 'No!'.
I'll ask Lucrèce's father for her hand,
But no more obstacles - you understand?

DORANTE: I'm coming with you.

GERONTE: No. Stay where you are.
Perhaps I'm taking tolerance too far -
But let me make this absolutely clear:
There's to be NO MORE LYING - do you hear?
And if there is, I swear I'll cut you off
Without a sou. I think I've said enough.

Exit.

DORANTE: I know he'd never carry out that threat.

CLITON: You shouldn't have been honest with him yet.
You've done extremely well - you've fooled him twice -
But even so, a hat-trick would be nice.

DORANTE: I've had enough of your frivolity.
Besides, there's something else that's troubling me.

CLITON: This taste of truth is making you feel sick?
Or are you thinking up another trick?
I don't believe you really love Lucrèce,
And you're so full of cunning and caprice
That I'm inclined to take each word you say
And twist its meaning round the other way.

DORANTE: I love Lucrèce – of that you can be sure –
What bothers me is that it's not secure:
For one thing, if our fathers can't agree
It's over – but suppose they can, and she
Decides against me – what would I do then?
No one can take her place . . . but, there again,
Her friend's not bad: I saw them both just now –
I have to tell you, I've been wondering how
Her beauty slipped my notice yesterday.
My passion doesn't seem to know which way
To turn: I'm meant to be Lucrèce's slave,
But now I don't know who I'd rather have!

CLITON: If you're not certain of your love for her,
Why did you tell your father that you were?

DORANTE: Loving one girl makes sense – it wouldn't do
To tell him I was half in love with two.

CLITON: Even to tell the truth you have to lie!

DORANTE: It was the only way to pacify
The man. I'd like to find out how he knew –
God help whoever told him, when I do!
That bogus marriage was a brilliant ruse –
It would have left me ample time to choose
Between the two.

CLITON: You seem to've forgotten –
Clarice is marrying Alcippe – she's not on
The market any more.

DORANTE: That's true – she's not.

CLITON: Which makes Lucrèce the only choice you've got.

DORANTE: Alcippe's quite welcome to Clarice – he's earned her –
And I can always tell myself I spurned her.

I've given my affections too much rein,
But now they've settled on Lucrèce again.
Here comes that maid.

Enter Sabine.

You gave Lucrèce my letter?

SABINE: I did sir . . . but. . . .

DORANTE: "But" what? Did it upset her?

SABINE: She tore it up.

DORANTE: What?! Without reading it?

SABINE: 'Fraid so.

DORANTE: You didn't even have the wit
To make her open it?

SABINE: You should've seen
The way she scolded me – I might've been
Dismissed. . . .

DORANTE: I'm sure she'll make it up to you.
But in the meantime this will have to do.

He offers her another purse.

SABINE: I can't. . . .

DORANTE: I want to give it one more try.
My motto's always been 'Never say die.'

CLITON: *(To Dorante.)* She's acting up again. This golden bait
Is bound to catch her pretty soon – just wait.
She'll tell you everything before we're through.

DORANTE: You say she didn't read it – is that true?

SABINE: To be more accurate that's what she said
To tell you.

DORANTE: Well, let's have the truth instead.

Drops more money into the purse, which Sabine now takes.

CLITON: She's brilliant!

SABINE: I wouldn't have the gall.
To lie to you, monsieur – she read it all.

DORANTE: She doesn't hate me, then?

SABINE: Hate you?! What for?

DORANTE: Is she in love with me?

SABINE: Not yet.

DORANTE: You're sure?

SABINE: Positive.

DORANTE: Then there's someone else?

SABINE: I doubt it. . . .

DORANTE: I've got a chance?

SABINE: What would I know about it?

DORANTE: Please tell me. . . .

SABINE: Tell you what?

DORANTE: *(Searches for a last gold coin and reluctantly hands it over.)*
The facts.

SABINE: All right.

DORANTE: D'you think she'll fall in love with me?

SABINE: She might.

DORANTE: But when?

SABINE: When she can trust you – not before.

DORANTE: But what if I'm not lying any more?

SABINE: If that's the case, then you can safely say
She's yours.

DORANTE: Good! Excellent! You've made my day.

SABINE: I have?

DORANTE: You told me she's in love with me.

SABINE: I did?

DORANTE: She's got to trust me now, you see:
My father. . . .

SABINE: Here she comes now, with Clarice.

Enter Clarice and Lucrèce.

CLARICE: *(To Lucrèce.)* There he is now. Remember my advice:
You'll have to tread extremely carefully.

DORANTE: *(To Clarice.)*
I'm yours, Lucrèce. What will you do with me?

CLARICE: *(To Lucrèce.)* He's looking straight at *me*! I wonder why.

LUCRECE: *(To Clarice.)*
That doesn't mean a thing . . . perhaps he's shy.

They exchange a doubtful look.

DORANTE: *(To Clarice.)* My life revolves around you – you're my sun.
When you're not shining on me, I'm undone!
I never dreamed that love could have such power –
Each minute you're away feels like an hour –
Each hour a year!

CLARICE: *(To Lucrèce.)* It's *me* he's looking at!

LUCRECE: *(To Clarice.)*
But here's his letter – what d'you make of that?

CLARICE: *(To Lucrèce.)* Just listen to the man!

LUCRECE: You've got it wrong.
It's *me* he's talking to.

CLARICE: *(To Lucrèce.)* It won't take long
To sort this out. *(To Dorante.)* Monsieur, might I enquire
Who is the object of this wild desire?

DORANTE: You are, although desire makes little sense.
When faced with such complete intransigence.

CLARICE: *(To Lucrèce.)* Either he talks in a peculiar way,
Or he's addressing me – which would you say?

LUCRECE: *(To Clarice.)* I'm mystified.

CLARICE: *(To Lucrèce.)* Let's hear him out, and see
The full extent of his duplicity.

LUCRECE: *(To Clarice.)* Such blatant fickleness just doesn't pay.

CLARICE: *(To Lucrèce.)* He worships you by night, and me by day!
(To Dorante.) Monsieur, I wonder if you recognise me?

DORANTE: What?! Are you trying to antagonise me?
Didn't I meet you in the Tuileries?
Didn't I opt for instant slavery?

CLARICE: If what my friend here tells me is correct,
A second passion's caused you to neglect
The first.

DORANTE: What utter rubbish! Neglect *you*?
I'll tear my heart out first, and eat it, too!

CLARICE: But aren't you married?

DORANTE: No, of course I'm not.
Are you two making fun of me, or what?
I've told you once: that "marriage" was a ruse
To keep me free for you.

CLARICE: Which would you choose:
An Ethiope, an English girl, or me?

DORANTE: Look, all I want is you – quite honestly,
You could be pink and green, for all I care.
English is stretching it a bit – be fair!

CLARICE: And yet, you're quite indifferent to Clarice?

DORANTE: Of course I am – this web of artifice –
I wove it all for you – devised each ruse
For you.

CLARICE: Well, now I'm totally confused!
Lucrèce, a word. . . .

DORANTE: What's that? "LUCRECE, A WORD"!!??
(To Cliton.) She just called *her* Lucrèce!

CLITON: I know. I heard.
Then I was right about their names, although
It's not my place to say "I told you so".

DORANTE: But then, last night. . . ?

CLITON: I know! *She* took *her* place.
It being dark, you couldn't see her face.

DORANTE: OF COURSE! *(Thinks.)*
But my affections were unsteady,
And fresh desires had stirred in me already –
In fact, I've merely travelled, without knowing,

To where my heart's already thought of going!
In view of which, why give the game away?
Just stand aside and watch – I'm going to play
My best trick yet.

CLARICE: *(To Lucrèce.)* Let's see how far he goes.

LUCRECE: It's really going to hit him when he knows
How he's been tricked.

CLARICE: *(To Dorante.)* Monsieur, my friend and I
Have been conferring, and we're wondering why
You courted *her* last night, and spoke of *me*,
To say the least, rather dismissively.

DORANTE: I love her but I've never courted her.

CLARICE: Of course you have – last night.

DORANTE: *(Heavy mock realisation.)* AH!!! You refer
To that transparent trick you played on me?
You took her place and hoped I wouldn't see –
But, honestly, it's such an old routine –
You didn't really think it took me in?

CLARICE: *(To Lucrèce.)* Is this the truth at last?

DORANTE: In fact, I've played
A better game than you – your masquerade
Backfired – to punish your duplicity
I made a show of gullibility.
He who laughs last . . . Next time you'd better choose
An easier victim, or you're bound to lose.
But you're the one I love – the years I've spent
Without you seem like one long punishment.

LUCRECE: *(Exasperated)* If you love *her*, what was this letter for?
(Shows him the note.)

DORANTE: *(To Lucrèce.)*
Sweet lady! Nothing could have pleased me more
Than that reaction! You're in love with me!
That was my final piece of trickery –
Clarice – I mean Lucrèce – it's *you* I love.

CLARICE: *(Disgusted)* The man's despicable! Good God above!

DORANTE: Please, ladies, if you'll only hear me out,
I'll put an end to any further doubt.

(*To Lucrèce.*) I came for you and got Clarice instead –
I realised what was happening, as I've said,
But, wounded though I was to think that you
Could trifle with my love, I saw it through.

LUCRECE: And when you wooed her in the Tuileries?

DORANTE: Merely a harmless piece of flattery
To make you jealous –

CLARICE: This is simply vile!

DORANTE: (*To Lucrèce.*) I may have talked to *her*, but all the while
My love for *you* was raging in my heart.
In short, it's you I've wanted from the start.
I only kept it quiet till I knew
Whether my father would approve of you.

CLARICE: Trick after trick, and fiction after fiction.
Playing with women's hearts – it's an addiction!

DORANTE: My own heart's lying at Lucrèce's feet.

CLARICE: Pooh! I can smell the treachery and deceit!

DORANTE: (*To Lucrèce.*) And if I told you that our fathers were
Discussing matters, would you still demur?

LUCRECE: That would depend on whether it was true –
But if it was, I might consider you.

DORANTE: I thought as much. We haven't long to wait.
Meanwhile, cheer up, Clarice – you've got your mate;
Here he comes now.

CLITON: Here comes your father, too

DORANTE: A happy ending! Everyone's on cue!

Enter Alcippe and Géronte.

ALCIPPE: (*To Clarice.*) Clarice, our fathers have agreed – it's done!

GERONTE: (*To Lucrèce.*) Lucrèce, your father's happy with my son.

DORANTE: (*To Lucrèce.*)
One word from those sweet lips, and you'll become
My wife. (*Pause*) Well? What's the matter? Are you dumb?

LUCRECE: If it's my father's wish, I must obey.

CLARICE: I feel the same – there's nothing more to say!
Lucrèce, let's go and read some poetry.

Exeunt Clarice and Lucrèce, laughing.

ALCIPPE: How can she treat it all so flippantly?
I'm going after her, if you'll excuse me.

Exit.

GERONTE: I never thought that marriage would amuse me –
But this has proved me wrong – tremendous stuff!
Dorante, I'm going home to sleep it off.

Exit.

SABINE: *(To Dorante.)*
Monsieur, it never rains gold but it pours. . . .

DORANTE: Take this.

He turns out his pockets and drops a final, tiny coin into her hand.

SABINE: I couldn't. . . .

DORANTE: I insist – it's yours.

Sabine drops the coin into her purse and exit.

Now, I suppose *I* really ought to go
And find my wife.

CLITON: *(Calling after him.)* Which one? Or don't you know?

(To audience.)

Liars get into scrapes, but there's no doubt
They're also pretty good at getting out!
And if you found the whole thing mystifying,
Take my advice, and brush up on your lying.

THE END

THE ILLUSION

CHARACTERS

ALCANDRE (A magician)

PRIDAMANT (Clindor's father)

DORANTE (Pridamant's friend)

MATAMORE (A captain, in love with Isabelle)

CLINDOR (The captain's servant, also in love with Isabelle)

ADRASTE (A gentleman, in love with Isabelle)

GERONTE (Isabelle's father)

ISABELLE (Géronte's daughter, in love with Clindor)

LISE (Isabelle's maid)

ERASTE (Florilame's servant)

GAOLER

PAGE

SERVANTS

ACT ONE

Dorante, Pridamant.

DORANTE: This is the place – this dark and desolate cave
Houses the man whose art has made a slave
Of Nature. Scarcely fitting, one might say,
For someone of his powers! The light of day
Is here diluted to a feeble glow,
Leaving the spirits free to come and go.

PRIDAMANT: My case is past all hope – my eagerness
To see him is the fruit of sheer distress.

He takes a few steps towards the cave entrance.

DORANTE: Don't move! Unless, of course, you want to die!
The air itself opposes all who try
To enter, hardening to bar their way;
He'll summon clouds of magic dust to play
A deadly game around your feet! He sees
Even the curious as enemies:
Waking him at an inauspicious hour
Is no less grave than challenging his power –
The punishment's the same, and everyone
Who wishes to consult him waits upon
His leisure. But the daily hour draws near
When, to amuse himself, he *does* appear.

PRIDAMANT: But can he use his powers to find my son –
Undo what my intransigence has done?
I criticised the boy – attempted, through
A father's harsh prerogative, to subdue
The natural wildness in him; but instead
Of bending to my will, he turned and fled!
Ten years I've scoured the world for him – in vain:
He swore to me we'd never meet again.
What a reversal! To mistreat one's son
While he's at home, and love him when he's gone!
Fatherly feelings came to me too late,
But I have seen the world, at any rate:
The Rhine, the Meuse, the Tagus and the Po –
I've crossed them all, and everywhere I go
I keep the image of him in my mind.
However, as I said, I've yet to find

A trace of the original. What's more,
I've had recourse to the black arts before –
Consulted wizards of no less renown
Than this Alcandre, and all have let me down.
The Underworld declines to answer me –
Or rather, answers, but with mockery.

DORANTE: Don't bracket him with lesser men like these –
Even in wizardry there are degrees.
The fact that he commands the lightning, or
Can bid the ocean overrun the shore
And summon earthquakes; that the winds will rise
In stormy ranks against his enemies;
That, on his lips, mysterious spells can rend
Great rocks, or make the thunder-clouds descend,
Or cause twin suns to shine at dead of night –
Such marvels needn't interest you. What might
Is his ability to read men's minds;
To see the future and the past; he finds
Nothing in all the universe arcane:
The course of Destiny, the human brain –
These are like open books to him. I, too,
Was sceptical, until I found he knew
The smallest details of my life – I heard
Forgotten loves rehearsed, each faltering word,
Each passionate sigh. . . .

PRIDAMANT: *(Drily)* You're claiming quite a lot.

DORANTE: But that's not all. . . .

PRIDAMANT: Enough! Like it or not,
Nothing but death can end my misery.

DORANTE: I've lived down here since leaving Britanny –
Managing my estates – I've yet to see
Someone consult Alcandre and come away
Unsatisfied. What's more, I'm bound to say
That in my own encounters with the man
I've always found him kind, and if I can
I'll use my influence to obtain for you
A similar response.

PRIDAMANT: Suppose you do –
If he can "read the book of Fate", he'll find
That Fate detests me above all mankind.

DORANTE: You're wrong – the end to your despair is here:
Alcandre has left the cave – he's drawing near.
See how his art, in its effects sublime,
Has not been used to check the work of time:
Sinew and bone are all that's left of him –
And yet, the movements light, the carriage straight,
Advancing easily, with even gait,
A hidden force informing every part,
Making each step a miracle of art.

Enter Alcandre.

Magus, whose studious toil, by night, gives way
To a fresh spate of miracles each day –
Omniscient, you divine our plans and view,
Though hidden from us, everything we do –
Your powers have worked on my behalf before,
I ask you now to marshal them once more
To help this poor old man, whose misery
I feel as though it were my own, since he
Was once a second father to me, and
His son, now lost, became my dearest friend.
If. . . .

ALCANDRE: Stop! I know exactly why you're here:
This Pridamant, unnaturally severe,
First drove his son away and now, too late,
Regrets his harshness and bemoans his fate.
In utter hopelessness he's come to me.

PRIDAMANT: Magus, I shan't repeat my history,
Since everything is known to you. Instead,
Let years of suffering move you, as they plead
For pity and assistance; let these tears
Win back the comfort of my failing years.
If he's alive, and you know where, one clue
Is all I dare, or need, to ask of you:
Give me the merest hint – no matter where,
Love will supply the wings to take me there.

ALCANDRE: Prepare to see him now: my art can bring
What Heaven has denied your suffering –
Before your very eyes, I shall present
The happy sequel to his banishment.
I tell you that you'll see your son again,

Honoured, magnificent, in exile. When
I speak, I act – for my young neighbour's sake
(Indicating Dorante.)
I shall reveal what followed your mistake.
The "wizards" you've consulted in the past
Have very little power – they should be classed
As mountebanks – their weird and wordy spells,
Their puffs of smoke, their herbs, their smells and bells –
The rites for which they make such dazzling claims –
Are nothing but a rigmarole, which aims
To make them seem far grander than they are,
And to scare you. More potency, by far,
Lies in this staff of mine, and to astound
My audience I merely strike the ground.

Alcandre strikes the ground with his staff, whereupon a dazzling array of costumes is revealed.

Judge your son's fortunes by this finery:
What prince was ever dressed more splendidly?

PRIDAMANT: Now I can see that you're deceiving me:
His sense of his own rank would not permit
My son to wear such clothes – I'm sure of it.

ALCANDRE: His fortunes have improved, and with them his
Assessment of his worth – the truth is this:
Your son's a person of some consequence –
No one could censure his magnificence.

PRIDAMANT: What stranger could be welcomer to me
Than hope?! Among the costumes there I see
A woman's – does this mean he has a wife?

ALCANDRE: I shall unfold the story of his life
And, if I felt that you were equal to it,
I'd conjure an illusion up to do it:
Some spirits, answering my call, would ape
The actors in his life – speech, gesture, shape
Fitting exactly with the parts they played.

PRIDAMANT: Then call them up at once – I'm not afraid:
To look upon his image holds no fears –
My mind's eye's looked on little else for years!

ALCANDRE: Then I must ask our noble friend to go:
What follows is for you alone. . . .

PRIDAMANT: How so?
There are no secrets between him and me. . . .

DORANTE: You must obey Alcandre unquestioningly –
I'll wait for you at home.

ALCANDRE: *(To Dorante.)* You'll meet again
Tonight – he'll tell you all about it then.

Exit Dorante.

Your son's was scarcely an immediate rise,
And to present his life for other eyes
Than yours would not have been appropriate.
There were some touches of the reprobate
In his behaviour. Just before he left
He stole some money from you, but the theft
Furnished him with a day or two's supplies,
If that, and soon he had to improvise:
While on the road, he earned a crust by selling
Quacksalves – he even did some fortune-telling!
He got to Paris, where he made his way
As many do, living from day to day.
He started with some secretarial work –
Rose to the lofty rank of lawyer's clerk –
But tired of it, and took to scribbling
Cheap ditties for the vagabonds to sing.
His style grew more ornate as time went on –
He churned out novels, epigrams, chansons,
Until at length his muse was quite worn out.
Then, not to be deterred, he set about
Dispensing balms, and plied a dubious trade
In so-called "medicines" such as mithridate.
When that failed, he became an advocate.
In short, one might have justly dubbed your son
A second Proteus – a chameleon
In human shape!

PRIDAMANT: It seems I'm in your debt
For keeping this between us two. . .

ALCANDRE: And yet,
In the sad catalogue I've just rehearsed,
To spare your feelings, I suppressed the worst.
The less the poor boy reaped, the more he'd sow –
Forever planting, seeing nothing grow,

Till his luck changed and took him to Bordeaux.
There, as he contemplated his next move,
One of the local bloods, who was in love,
Commissioned him to act as go-between.
And here our tale begins – to set the scene:
He proves an adept in this gentle art,
Supplants his master in the lady's heart,
And earns himself a lot of money, too.
Such are the intrigues I'll reveal to you,
Before I bring the story up to date,
And show him in his present, glorious state.

PRIDAMANT: I think there's something to be said for "art" –
It's nice to know the ending at the start!

ALCANDRE: One further detail to be watchful for –
Your son has changed his name – it's not Clindor,
But La Montagne. And lastly, please keep calm,
Though what ensues may cause you some alarm.
If I've delayed thus far, the reason is
That spirits such as those whose services
I now require, are only summoned by
Spells of extraordinary potency.
Now, come into the cave, where I'll prepare
A charm to conjure actors out of air!

They enter the cave.

END OF ACT ONE

ACT TWO

Alcandre, Pridamant.

ALCANDRE: Don't leave the cave unless I tell you to,
For certain death awaits you if you do.

Two phantoms appear in the guises of Clindor and Matamore.

The phantom that impersonates your son
Is here. And that's his master.

PRIDAMANT: It's begun!
I want to touch him. . . .

ALCANDRE: Listen quietly!

Alcandre draws Pridamant to one side as Clindor and Matamore enter.

CLINDOR: You're deep in contemplation – could it be
That, not content with countless glorious deeds,
Your valour mocks the meat on which it feeds?

MATAMORE: Pardon?

CLINDOR: You're spoiling for a scrap.

MATAMORE: That's right –
Which of them do you think I ought to fight –
The Sophy, or the Mogul?

CLINDOR: Let them go!
Be merciful! How could their overthrow
Enhance a fame already so complete?
You'd need an army, too, for such a feat. . . .

MATAMORE: Nonsense! This arm of mine is strong enough –
I'll take them on alone, and see them off:
The very mention of my name can make
Ramparts collapse and massed batallions quake;
In fact, I'd barely need to rouse myself
To strip those princes of their power and wealth –
I'd only have to blow. . . .

CLINDOR: To blow?

MATAMORE: My breath
Is capable of scattering instant death!
The thunder is my cannon, Destiny
My standard-bearer, and you talk to *me*
Of armies!

Quite suddenly, he becomes calm.

Ah! A sudden, amorous thought
Has swooped on me, and made my mind its sport!
Her image causes anger to subside
And drives away all thoughts of homicide!
Her whim disposes of my liberty –
Cupid, who governs all, must govern me!
Witness the transformation in my face,
As bestial rage gives way to manly grace!

CLINDOR: Extraordinary! It seems that Cupid can
Transform you from a monster to a man –
And what a man! Unless I'm wholly wrong,
No woman could resist your charms for long.

MATAMORE: I can be anything I choose to be:
A wolf, a lamb, it's all the same to me –
As whim dictates, I'll tear a man apart
Or melt some unsuspecting woman's heart.
I had to cultivate my brutal side
To stop the ladies pestering me – they tried
To touch me everywhere I went – as soon
As I appeared they'd go berserk, or swoon!
Life was impossible – queens and princesses
Held me to ransom for my own caresses;
In short, from Ethiopia to Japan,
I was the archetypal ladies' man;
In Turkey several beauties, hoping to. . . .
Liaise with me, left the Seraglio
And got me into trouble with the Sultan.

CLINDOR: Such trouble one's entitled to exult in!

MATAMORE: But these activities distracted me
From wars of conquest, and eventually,
Exhausted, I instructed Destiny
To visit heaven and demand of Jove
Some respite from this unremitting love;
I strengthened my petition with a threat

To oust the mighty Thunderer from his seat
And give his bolts to Mars. In mortal, or
Rather, immortal fear, Heaven's governor
Granted my suit. Since then, as you can see,
I'm only handsome when I choose to be!

CLINDOR: It's just as well, or I'd be bringing you
Wave upon wave of tiresome *billets-doux!*

MATAMORE: Refuse them all, no matter from whose hand –
Other than hers, of course – you understand?
What does she think of me?

CLINDOR: She can't decide
Whether she's overjoyed or petrified –
She says you're like a human meteorite:
The terror of the earth, and its delight –
But if you really mean what you profess,
No goddess will have known such happiness.

MATAMORE: Goddesses have succumbed to me as well.

CLINDOR: They have?!

MATAMORE: There are some stories I could tell. . . .
On one occasion – possibly the first
Ever – the course of Nature was reversed:
The sun – a god revealed to mortal eyes –
Worshipped throughout the world – had failed to rise;
Nor could he cross the sky without Aurore,
The goddess of the dawn, to go before.
They hunted for her in the forested
Estates of Cephalus, the watery bed
Of old Tithonus, and the royal keep
Of Memnon, where she has been known to sleep,
But neither husband, son nor lover knew
Where Dawn had gone, and half the world made do
With lamps till noon.

CLINDOR: Amazing! Where did she
Eventually turn up?

MATAMORE: In bed with me!

CLINDOR: Of course! I was in darkest Mexico –
Stories about you reached me, even so –
Wasn't it Persia who upbraided you
For angering her favourite god?

MATAMORE: It's true:
A war was brewing, but I had to wait
To meet the Transylvanian delegate –
I had a quarrel with that insolent nation,
But dropped it when they offered reparation. . . .

CLINDOR: Mercy becomes the mighty!

MATAMORE: Look at me –
This face of mine is like an ABC
Of virtue – quick to subjugate the proud,
I spare the meek – my vassals are allowed
To rule their lands in peace: the civilised
Monarchs of Europe I have not chastised,
But those of Africa have frequently
Incurred my anger with their vanity –
Once, the Sahara was a fertile and
Populous country – it was this right hand,
Lifted in awful wrath, that laid it waste. . . .

CLINDOR: Here comes your mistress. . . .

MATAMORE: Damn! She's with Adraste!

Matamore makes to leave as Adraste and Isabelle, engaged in earnest conversation, enter.

CLINDOR: Where are you running off to?

MATAMORE: If I stay
He's bound to pick a quarrel – it's his way
Of showing off to her.

CLINDOR: Would that be wise?
You're sure to pulverise him if he tries. . . .

MATAMORE: I thought I told you, when my looks and charm
Are on display it's women I disarm,
Not men.

CLINDOR: Why not be less attractive, then –
Just turn yourself into a wolf again.

MATAMORE: With power like mine, it's hard to be exact. . . .
To destroy him, while leaving her intact. . . .
Out of the question! No – we'd better wait
In hiding, till they choose to separate.

CLINDOR: Courage *and* prudence – what a combination!

They conceal themselves.

ADRASTE: If this is how you feel, my situation
Seems hopeless – sighs and transports fail to move you –
You still refuse to see how much I love you.

ISABELLE: Refuse to see it! On the contrary:
I'm lovely, and you love me – what could be
Clearer than that? If there was any doubt,
"Transports and sighs" must surely rule it out.
Besides, I've always thought it quite absurd
Not to take men of honour at their word.
But women can behave with honour, too:
You're frank with me, so I'll be frank with you –
You can love on, as far as I'm concerned,
But don't expect your love to be returned.

ADRASTE: My ardour must have caused you grave offence
To earn me such a grudging recompense:
Sighs met with sneers and constancy with scorn. . . .

ISABELLE: What seems a rose to you may prove a thorn
To me: the point of view determines all –
This "love" and "constancy" of yours, I call
Obstinacy, or even persecution –
Language creates all manner of confusion –
There's something predatory in predilection,
And lovers can afflict us with affection!

ADRASTE: But love is sacred, and it's blasphemy
To treat a lover the way you treat me!
God made me with a single end in view:
My only function is to worship you!
Your beauty was my soul's efficient cause:
Even before I met you I was yours!
I've only offered you what's yours by right. . . .

ISABELLE: I'm not about to claim it! Let me cite
Another of God's *fiats*: I was sent
Into the world to treat you with contempt –
We should obey His wishes, shouldn't we?
You in particular: it's plain to see
He's got some grudge against you as it is –
Why else is He tormenting you like this
With unrequited love?

ADRASTE: Then you're aware
Of what I'm going through – you just don't care?

ISABELLE: You're wrong – I pity you – it gives me pain
To see you suffering like this in vain –
Obstinacy has its pathetic side.

ADRASTE: Your father favours me – what he decides
Is final. . . .

ISABELLE: What a conquest that would be –
To whisk me off on his authority!

ADRASTE: Since love has failed, we'll see what force can do.
This very day I mean to capture you.

ISABELLE: Oh yes? This very day I hope to see
A lover thwarted by calamity.

ADRASTE: Will this cascade of hatred never cease?

ISABELLE: Go to my father, and leave me in peace!

Adraste exits. Once he has gone, Matamore comes forward, followed by Clindor.

MATAMORE: Hardly a worthy rival, would you say?
As soon as I appeared he ran away!

ISABELLE: How can you blame him? Kings have done the same.
Such is the impact of your awesome fame.
But is that very fame deceiving me
With wonders that I only think I see?

MATAMORE: To end all doubt, accept me now and you'll
Receive a choice of territories to rule. . . .

CLINDOR: If you're not happy with the current batch,
He'll build an empire just for you, from scratch!

ISABELLE: *(To Matamore.)*
Why waste your powers on gifts I don't require?
To serve your wishes is my sole desire.

MATAMORE: My wishes wait on yours: at your command,
I am prepared to stay this conquering hand,
And give my vassals back their sovereignty –
I'd keep a prince or two to wait on me,
Or hand you *billets-doux* on bended knee. . . .

ISABELLE: Think of the jealousy I might incur
When people saw your royal messenger –
Amorous dealings ought to be discreet –
(Indicates Clindor.)
A go-between like him is all we need.

MATAMORE: How right you are! You seem to share with me
A natural reticence and modesty!
These days, I find that conquered kingdoms lack
Their old appeal – I often give them back
As soon as they submit; princesses, too,
Have lost their charm – why should I stoop to woo
A lady who's no sooner wooed than won?

ISABELLE: Now, there's a point I'd like to quiz you on:
I can't believe I've won a heart that's been
Denied to duchesses, and cold to queens!

MATAMORE: Ask him. *(Indicates Clindor.)*
(To Clindor.) Tell her about the tournament
That made me famous in the Orient,
When I wrought havoc in the lists, before
The daughters of the Chinese emperor. . . .

CLINDOR: They fell in love with him, but were denied –
Both, in their grief, committed suicide.
I was in Egypt then, but even there
The man was being talked of everywhere –
He'd lately taken Cairo, put to rout
Some ogres, conquered countries round about,
Flattened two mountains, razed a dozen forts,
Set fire to settlements of every sort,
Besieged Damascus for a while, and then
Made mincemeat of a hundred thousand men!

MATAMORE: He's got the sequence of events off pat –
I'd actually forgotten most of that.

ISABELLE: Can such prodigious exploits slip your mind?

MATAMORE: Prodigious! They were nothing of the kind!
The subjugation of those lesser breeds
I count among my least momentous deeds.

Enter page, sheepishly.

MATAMORE: What is it? Speak up!

PAGE: An ambassador. . . .

MATAMORE: Indeed? From whom?

PAGE: The Queen of England, sir.

MATAMORE: Again! She needs less beauty and more sense.

The page hands him a letter, which he peruses cursorily.

The answer is: complete indifference.

Exit page.

CLINDOR: *(To Isabelle.)* He spurns the Queen of England for your sake!

ISABELLE: Yes! It's a compliment, and no mistake!

The page re-enters and whispers in Matamore's ear.

MATAMORE: *(To page.)* She's an incorrigible optimist!
It's absolutely pointless to persist.
Say: if she really wants me to upset her,
I'll clarify my feelings in a letter.

The page exits, as before.

I have to leave you for a while – this man
Has been my closest confidant and can,
I'm sure, dispel such doubts as you may have
About the conqueror who's now your slave.

ISABELLE: Don't be too long – the sooner you're back here,
The greater your devotion will appear.

Exit Matamore.

CLINDOR: That was a piece of vintage Matamore:
His page announces an "ambassador",
So-called, and off he rushes to "upset"
A monarch that he's never even met!

ISABELLE: His antics pleased me better than he knew –
The madman's gone, and I'm alone with you.

CLINDOR: Hearing you talk like that emboldens me
To seize upon this opportunity. . . .

A pause.

ISABELLE: Well? Seize away!

CLINDOR: I love you. . . . you're my heart,
My soul. . . . without your love I'll fall apart!
My life. . . .

ISABELLE: Love oughtn't to be overstated;
Nor can you doubt that it's reciprocated:
(Laughingly) Only consider what I've just turned down –
Two suitors, *and* the offer of a crown!
I say I love you, and those simple words
Suffice – devotion should be felt, not heard –
If we're in love, a glance can do the rest –
Nothing is said, but volumes are expressed.

CLINDOR: I should have known that Love would treat me well:
The other gods have made me go through Hell!
In exile here, with neither means nor friends,
Reduced to furthering the futile ends
Of this – this popinjay! – in my despair,
I find a girl who doesn't seem to care
For wealth or grandeur – who can laugh at Fate
And love me, even in my wretched state.

ISABELLE: Of course! How else should such a choice be made?
A love returned is more than amply paid.
Cupid is blind – to what he stands to lose;
Love keeps no score of wrongs – or revenues!
My father doesn't share this point of view:
Let him disown me, then – I must have you.

CLINDOR: Such love! For one so undeserving. . . . so. . . .

ISABELLE: Here comes Adraste again! I'd better go!

Exit.

ADRASTE: *(Entering)* Only your luck can match my misery:
She talks to you – she runs away from me!
Though, looking at the thing a different way:
You haven't got the charm to make her stay
With me about!

CLINDOR: So bitter! Without cause:
It was my fault she ran away, not yours.

ADRASTE: What do you mean?

CLINDOR: This suit of Matamore's –
She's sick of it: he triumphs, in his head,
By sea, by land, in Heaven and in bed!

ADRASTE: Well, if you can't control these flights of his,
How about channelling his energies
Elsewhere?

CLINDOR: What sort of threat can he present?
To you? He woos her like a battlement!
Lays at her feet a corpse, a city sacked,
"Batallions" massacred, limbs freshly hacked!

ADRASTE: It's quite grotesque – you don't imagine he
Could possibly arouse my jealousy?
You, on the other hand, are not the man
To serve that lunatic without some plan.
Since you arrived in town, her attitude
To me has grown decidedly subdued –
I'm starting to suspect you of foul play:
Either you're in some other rival's pay,
Or else you're tired of wooing to command,
Preferring to attempt it at first hand.
Anyway, you can tell this Matamore
To find himself another mistress, or,
If Isabelle must be his fancy's queen,
To hire a less. . . . proficient go-between!
Not that I'm anxious – there can only be
One outcome, since her father favours me –
It lies with you to rid me of a pest,
And you'd be wise to do as I suggest –
I warn you, if I catch you here again,
We'll have to settle this affair like men!

CLINDOR: I wouldn't dream of getting in your way. . .

ADRASTE: Then leave Bordeaux – that's all I have to say!

CLINDOR: Whatever you perceive to be my fault,
I can't believe it warrants this assault.
Now, your blood may be blue, and mine plain red,
But I've as much of it as you to shed,
If honour calls for it.

ADRASTE: What's that? A threat?!
From you?!

CLINDOR: Before I've finished, you'll regret
That arrogance of yours. . . .

Adraste draws.

. . . but not just yet!

Clindor exits hurriedly.

Enter Lyse.

ADRASTE: His insolence is driving me insane!

LYSE: Aaah! Has he been upsetting you again?

ADRASTE: *(Dismayed to find that he has been overheard.)*
Upsetting?! Me?! I don't know what you mean.

LYSE: You're jealous – of the madman's go-between.

ADRASTE: Nonsense. It's all a matter of degree:
A valet more desirable than me?
Impossible. It's irritating, though,
To see the two of them conversing so. . . .

LYSE: Intimately? You see? You are upset.

ADRASTE: I'm not, but lovers have a right to fret:
Call me irrational. . . . call me a clown. . . .
I must know where I stand. . . .

LYSE: You've fallen down.

ADRASTE: Meaning?

LYSE: She is in love with him. It's true.
I've seen some doting couples, but THOSE TWO!
Like dogs on heat, they are!

ADRASTE: Ah! Isabelle!
Ungrateful, callous, TREACHEROUS JEZA. . . .

LYSE: Quite.

ADRASTE: To throw me over for a layabout!

LYSE: He claims he's rich – a gentleman. . . .

ADRASTE: A lout,
More like.

LYSE: He ran away from home, it seems –
Experimented with some crack-brained schemes,

Before he found himself employment here,
As postman to this balmy buccaneer.
Of course, the job provides the perfect cover:
He doubles, now, as messenger and lover.
He's cheated Matamore, and ousted you.
But don't you worry – all you have to do
Is call her father in. It won't take long
To make her understand she's in the wrong.

ADRASTE: I spoke with him just now, and I'm assured
My patience will receive its just reward.
Meanwhile, there's something you can help me with.

LYSE: I'm at your service.

ADRASTE: What I wouldn't give
To catch them. . . .

LYSE: In the act? As one might say?

ADRASTE: Exactly.

LYSE: I'll arrange it right away.

ADRASTE: Good girl. Here, take this ring – it's amethyst.

LYSE: But it's my pleasure. . . .

Adraste makes to pocket the ring again.

Well, if you insist!

She snatches the ring from him.

ADRASTE: And rest assured, we'll make him stew for this!

Exit Adraste.

LYSE: That puffed up little valet's going to see
What comes of playing cat and mouse with me.
He's got no business putting on such airs:
He's tried the pantry – now he's moved upstairs!
Just what gives him the right to pick and choose?
Charm and a pretty face? That's hardly news.
Looks don't entitle you to instant wealth:
I'm not exactly hideous myself!
As for the wandering nobleman routine,
It isn't hard to improvise: I mean –
The man's a total stranger in Bordeaux –
He could be Jesus Christ, for all we know!

Anyway, wandering nobleman or not,
The little rat's about to learn what's what!

Exit.

ALCANDRE: Your pulse is racing.

Pridamant checks this, confirming it with a resigned nod.

PRIDAMANT: What's she going to do?

ALCANDRE: She's much too fond of him to "make him stew".

PRIDAMANT: Hell hath no fury like a woman scorned. . . .

ALCANDRE: Her heart's not broken, though – it's merely torn.

END OF ACT TWO

ACT THREE

Enter Géronte, Isabelle.

GERONTE: I'm adamant – I thought I'd made that clear
These sighs and tears won't get you anywhere.
And though it pains me, seeing you like this,
I know I'm right – it's hard, but there it is.
What irks you is the fact that I know best –
Whoever I approved of, you'd detest.
Naturally, if I say Adraste's the man,
You'd rather marry an orang-utan!
He's handsome, charming, rich, of noble birth,
But no – your pride must blind you to his worth.

ISABELLE: He's the most eligible man on earth!
The trouble is, I'm not in love with him:
The Love-god lets his arrows fly at whim –
They drop on us, out of a clear blue sky,
And passion grips us – only Heaven knows why:
These matters are decided up above –
It's madness to oppose the power of love.

GERONTE: I've had my fill of truisms like these –
All that concern me are realities.
Who might your partner be in this romance?
Not Matamore, the Genghis Khan of France?
Well done! A psychopathic son-in-law!

ISABELLE: What kind of moron do you take me for?!

GERONTE: Who's instigated this rebellion, then?

ISABELLE: My peace of mind, my self-respect – not men!
You choose Adraste, and call it "marrying well",
Condemning me to spend my life in Hell!

GERONTE: Count yourself lucky he's content with you –
He could do better, if he wanted to.
For the last time, I wish it – now, obey!

ISABELLE: Test my obedience in some other way. . . .

GERONTE: Enough! My word is law! IT SHALL BE THUS!
Go in – there's nothing further to discuss.

Isabelle goes in.

What a display! Young people nowadays!
Where did they learn such disobedient ways?
For me, my father's word was holy writ,
And it was heresy to question it,
BUT NOW! It's arguments at every turn,
Especially where daughters are concerned!
Whatever plans for them you care to make,
They'll be opposed, for opposition's sake!
Well, Miss Caprice, I've gone on the attack –
The wisdom of the old is fighting back!
(Looking off.) Oh, not again! It's the mad musketeer!
God give me strength – or get him out of here!

Enter Matamore, with Clindor. Matamore makes sure Géronte is in earshot before speaking.

MATAMORE: Life's difficult for famous fighting men:
The Grand Vizir has sent for me again,
I've had a plea for help from Tartary,
And Calicut's again in need of me. . . .
What now? I can't divide myself in three!

CLINDOR: You can't? In that case, I should let them stew:
Help one, and you'll offend the other two. . . .
(He purses his lips, affecting to weigh it up.)
It's risky. . . .

MATAMORE: How I hate diplomacy!
The bedroom is the place for jealousy. . . .

He affects to notice Géronte.

Monsieur! Forgive my negligence! I swear,
I really didn't see you standing there.
You seem perturbed – you've made some enemy?
Pronounce his name and leave the rest to me!

GERONTE: Thank you – I've made no enemies . . . . as yet.

MATAMORE: But for this arm, you would have been beset
With them.

GERONTE: Indeed? Too kind of you, I'm sure.

MATAMORE: I've made our friendship known – you're quite secure.

GERONTE: Isn't your prowess rather wasted here?
What can Bordeaux offer the buccaneer?

You're hardly going to further your renown,
Twiddling your thumbs in a provincial town.
That sword of yours – what do you wear it for?
You're always rattling it, but never draw –
Or that's what people say. . . .

MATAMORE: Of course, you're right,
But what am I to do? My hands are tied
By love.

GERONTE: My daughter's all that's keeping you?
Then leave at once, and with my blessing, too:
She's spoken for.

MATAMORE: I don't know what you mean –
Haven't you heard? I'm making her a queen!

GERONTE: Now look, old chap – this conqueror routine –
Wouldn't you say it's wearing rather thin?
Be a good fellow, take your crown elsewhere –
My daughter doesn't want it – IS THAT CLEAR?

MATAMORE: Poor man! You've just condemned yourself to death.

GERONTE: Have I, indeed?

CLINDOR: He'll kill you with his breath.

GERONTE: Breathe on me, then. Let's see what you can do.
You'll have to breathe on all my servants, too.

MATAMORE: Tell him about the wonders I've performed.

CLINDOR: The wonders. . . . yes. . . .

GERONTE: I'm going . You've been warned.
It's nothing personal, you understand –
I'm tetchy, and the people I command
Are not imaginary – they're big, strong men!

Exit.

MATAMORE: I would have pulverised him, there and then,
But for the love of Isabelle. Ah, love!
How inconvenient you're apt to prove!
I could have faced a hundred rivals, rather
Than lay a finger on my mistress' father.
Why else would I, a mighty warrior, let
That fossil get away with such a threat?!

CLINDOR: Don't worry. Now's your chance. While he's away,
Press home your suit – propose to her today.

MATAMORE: By Jove! But what about those big strong men?

CLINDOR: That sword of yours'll soon take care of them.

MATAMORE: I daren't unleash more power than I require –
One flash of this could set their house on fire:
Ridge, tile and rafter, batten, slat and gutter,
Lath, transom, rail and joist, consigned to utter
Destruction, not to mention uprights, beams,
Scantlings and braces, swallowed in the flames.
Think of the columns, lintels, window-sills –
The jambs, the ledges, casements, doors and grilles –
Glass, marble, brick, cement, lead, iron, slate,
All sharing in a single fiery fate
With attics, bedrooms, atriums, as well as
Staircases, closets, balconies and cellars.
And wouldn't the effect of such a fire
Be to . . . extinguish Isabelle's desire?

CLINDOR: Hmmm . . . I imagine women tend to frown
On lovers, when they burn their houses down!

MATAMORE: No – somebody completely ordinary
Is what's required – you go and speak for me.

CLINDOR: Thank you, but won't. . . . ?

MATAMORE: There's someone coming out –
That little monster of a maid, no doubt.

He runs off.

CLINDOR: *(To audience.)* Warrior, indeed! A shadow's all it takes
To frighten him: a geriatric makes
An ass of him, he's constantly afraid
Of thrashings, and in terror of a maid!
(To Lyse.) How do you manage to inspire such dread?
The mighty Matamore just turned and fled!

LYSE: It's looks that do it: men can't get enough
Of CERTAIN faces – others scare them off.

CLINDOR: Repel the mad, since you delight the sane:
Heaven help other women, if you're plain!
You've all the graces: wit, intelligence,

Vivacity combined with common sense,
Doe eyes, fine features, fabulous complexion,
Fantastic figure – feminine perfection!

LYSE: When did you first observe these qualities?
This isn't Isabelle, you know, it's Lyse.

CLINDOR: If *she* possessed your power to bewitch –
Or if *your* father were extremely rich. . . .

LYSE: You're pretty fussy, but you'll have to choose,
And when you do, the witch is bound to lose.

CLINDOR: I fell for her because it paid me to,
Whereas I couldn't help but fall for you.
Love is its own reward – marriages need
All manner of incentives to succeed:
What are the things a man wants most in life?
Joy from a mistress, comfort from a wife.
You see, we're too alike – you're penniless,
And my affairs are in a total mess:
Passion is poisoned by necessity,
And love's no antidote to poverty.
But when I'm married, and my stock is high,
I'll think of you and heave a wistful sigh,
As I recall in what a brutal fashion
My reason went and trampled on my passion!

LYSE: Your least attractive feature is your wit –
Your mouth's quite nice until you open it.
These loving lectures I can do without,
And passion should be felt, not thought about.
I'm grateful to you, though, for saving me
From being "poisoned by necessity";
It's quite a sacrifice you've had to make,
Suffering wealth and status, for my sake!
I shan't forget it in a hurry. . . .

CLINDOR: *(Smiling)* Lyse!
How happy I could be with. . . .

LYSE: Drop it, please.
She's waiting. . . .

She gestures off, and up, in the direction of Isabelle's appartments.

CLINDOR: Will you banish me like this?

LYSE: That's right: I banish you - to wedded bliss!

CLINDOR: Your anger's irresistible!

LYSE: Just go!

CLINDOR: You understand my reasons?

LYSE: YES. I KNOW.
Nothing will come of nothing, but a pair
Of nothings leads to sorrow and despair.

CLINDOR: Goodbye, then - you can banter with such skill,
If I don't leave you now, I never will!

Exit.

LYSE: You bastard! To pretend to love someone
Because they're pretty, and it might be fun!
I suppose what I feel's irrelevant,
As long as you can play at being "gallant".
Opening your heart - to show me that it's false;
So hot for me you're marrying someone else!
Well, chop your heart in two (I wish you would) -
It isn't going to do you any good:
You wait until my mistress gets to hear
She's just a stepping stone in your career!
I "banter" with you, but it's all to hide
The hate and anger boiling up inside:
Revenge is hardly something you announce -
Panthers'll wait for hours before they pounce -
Setting a trap needs stealth, and careful thought -
I'm going to have a field-day when you're caught!

A mischievous chuckle mounts to evil laughter before subsiding, comically, into blubbering. She pulls out a handkerchief, blows her nose and addresses the audience.

But what's he done that I'm so furious at?
Feathered his nest? There's nothing wrong with that.
He does love me - he just loves money more -
These days, that's not worth hating someone for!
And then, all that about necessity:
There's something in it - should I leave him be?

I mean, if I love him, and I'm in Hell,
Since he loves me, he must be there as well!
The Bible says: "Love keeps no score of wrongs",
And it's with Isabelle that he belongs. . . .
Yes! I forgive him!

A pious simper gives way to a scowl, and she reproaches herself.

Lyse! What's wrong with you?
"Vengeance is mine." That's in the Bible, too!
He loves you, and he leaves you on the rocks –
You love him, and you're made a laughing stock!
If it was love that got you in this state,
What's going to get you out of it but hate?
When love turns sour, it brings its own rewards:
Revenge tastes even sweeter afterwards!

Exit, cackling.

Night is now falling, as Matamore makes his way with extreme caution down the aisle and across the stage.

MATAMORE: They're coming! False alarm. It's them – take cover!
No – just the wind. I'm trembl-ing all over!
Right – on we go. It's dark – I can't be seen.

He reaches that end of the stage where we take Isabelle's house to be.

Good. This is where I hope to meet my queen.
I'll show that dotard! But those men of his. . . .
I haven't been this scared for . . . centuries!
You see, I'm done for if they find me now:
Defend myself? I couldn't stoop that low –
Not against servants! Greatness can impose
Some oddly perilous restraints! Who knows –
If I could run for it, I might survive:
I'm probably the fastest man alive. *(Noises from house.)*
Well – here we go – the final sacrifice:
I can't run now, my legs have turned to ice!
Fates, cut the thread!

Sound of people approaching. Matamore crosses himself, closes his eyes and waits for death. We see Isabelle and Clindor in the gloom.

The Fates have changed their plan:
It's not those men – it's HER, and La Montagne.
My legs are thawing! I'll conceal myself,
And listen to him woo on my behalf.

Matamore hides as Isabelle and Clindor take the stage. They speak in hushed voices.

ISABELLE: Things don't look good on the paternal front:
I've never seen him so intransigent.
It seems that no one but Adraste will do –
Meanwhile, Adraste is getting awkward too.
That's why we have to meet out here – upstairs,
You're cornered if they catch us unawares.
I feel much happier on open ground. . . .

She conducts a brief reconnaissance, almost stumbling on Matamore in the process.

CLINDOR: You shouldn't take such pains on my account.

ISABELLE: How can you talk like that, when all I've done
Is to ensure the safety of someone
Whose love I value more than beauty, wealth,
All that the world can offer – life itself?

Matamore's interest is visibly roused.

Let Father do his worst – I'm adamant. . . .

MATAMORE: *(Aside)* Excellent!

ISABELLE: You're the only man I want.

MATAMORE: *(Aside)* What's that?!

ISABELLE: Whatever hardships Fortune sends,
I'll bear them, and be faithful to the end:
I'll suffer anything in such a cause –
Adraste's advances – even Matamore's.

MATAMORE: *(Aside)* Good God!

CLINDOR: *(To Isabelle.)* You're hurting me with happiness:
What man could ask for more, or merit less?
This is my wealth – this life –

A vague, contemptuous gesture indicates his current situation.

it scarcely buys
One look of kindness from those lovely eyes.
Some day, my star may change its influence –
Restore to me my lost inheritance –
If not, how can the sacrifice you've made
Ever be, even partially, repaid?
Of course my heart is cheered by what you've said,
But how can you deny that, as things stand,
Adraste, my rival, has the upper hand?
And the courageous words you're forced to eat
Will taste as bitter as they sounded sweet.

ISABELLE: You're wrong. This pessimism's premature.
You can be doubtful if you like – I'm sure.
You must be patient. . . .

MATAMORE: This is quite absurd!
(Emerging) I have to speak!

ISABELLE: Damn! We've been overheard.

CLINDOR: Our friend the conqueror – leave this to me. . . .

MATAMORE: Traitor!

CLINDOR: Talk quietly!

MATAMORE: TALK QUIETLY?!!!

CLINDOR: The servants. . . .

MATAMORE: What about them?

CLINDOR: Use your head:
If they come out, we're both as good as dead.

MATAMORE: This way. . . .

His caution reawakened, he drags Clindor across the stage.

You may as well confess your crime:
You've been . . . . cavorting with her, all this time!

CLINDOR: I've toyed with her, perhaps. Just harmless fun. . . .

MATAMORE: I kill in several different ways – which one
Would you prefer? A single, crushing blow?
Or slicing into little bits, like so?

He demonstrates with his sword.

Or I could bury you in the earth's core,
Or toss you, higher than a meteor,
To be consumed by elemental fire. . . .
Make your decision quickly, and expire!

CLINDOR: No. *I'll* give *you* a choice. . . .

MATAMORE: What might that be?

CLINDOR: To run for it, or to be thrashed by me.

MATAMORE: *(Aside)* Incredible! He should be on his knees,
Not trying to open the hostilities!
Unless. . . . Of course! It's a conspiracy!
He's in the old man's pay! You – come with me:
The oceans of the world are all my slaves –
I'll get them to engulf you in the waves!

CLINDOR: I have a less ambitious plan for you:
That stagnant pond behind the house should do!

MATAMORE: *(Aside)* Damnation! He's in league with them, all right!

CLINDOR: Look, I've already killed ten men tonight.
I'd make you the eleventh, willingly,
But. . . .

MATAMORE: *(Aside)* So! He's dabbling in butchery!
Serving a hero must have some effect –
Yes, if he'd shown a little more respect,
I'd have considered making him my squire. . . .
(To Clindor.) I'm not unreasonable – I've no desire
To kill so promising a duellist:
Why don't you ask my pardon, and desist
From these advances, which dishonour one
Whose love is mine by right, and mine alone?
I'm merciful as well as murderous. . . .

CLINDOR: Was there a passion more imperious?
Look, if the lady means so much to you,
Why don't you prove it, in a bout or two?

Draws.

MATAMORE: What pluck! What chivalry! It's most refreshing!
Continue your attentions, with my blessing!
Accept her – as a mark of gratitude.

CLINDOR: For what? My services?

MATAMORE: Your attitude.

CLINDOR: Saviour of kings! Model of power and grace –
May all the world re-echo with your praise!

Isabelle, who has been listening the while, now joins them.

ISABELLE: I'm overjoyed to see you're friends again.
(To Matamore.)
You're quite the most magnanimous of men!

MATAMORE: As you're aware, I'd previously planned
To honour you by asking for your hand:
I've changed my mind, but, if you're interested,
I offer you this gentleman instead:
I recommend him to you heartily –
He won his spurs while serving under me.

ISABELLE: I'll try to love him, for your sake.

CLINDOR: Of course,
We're counting on your secrecy. . . .

MATAMORE: It's yours –
And my protection, too: you'll open doors
Throughout the world, by mentioning my name –
From Paris to Peking its power's the same –
A talisman. . . .

ISABELLE: We'll try it.

CLINDOR: *(To Matamore.)* Now, a kiss –
With your permission – to confirm our bliss. . . .

MATAMORE: *(With great solemnity.)* Proceed.

Isabelle and Clindor kiss as Adraste enters, sword drawn.

ADRASTE: Enjoy it! It'll be your last!
(Calling off.) TREACHERY!

Géronte enters with a group of armed servants.

MATAMORE: This is happening too fast!
I function when I'm champing at the bit,
Or not at all – I'd better run for it!

He runs into the house, where Isabelle has already fled.

Meanwhile, Clindor fights his way through the group of servants, to confront Adraste.

CLINDOR: Feel safer in a pack? You jackal, you!
I've sought you out, and now I'll run you through!

They fight. Virtually at once, Clindor wounds Adraste.

GERONTE: Adraste's been wounded. Fetch a doctor! Quick!
And someone apprehend that lunatic!

CLINDOR: It's no use. I'm outnumbered. Isabelle!
Fate is a pit – I've fallen in – farewell!

GERONTE: To prison with him! And the rest of you,
Carry Adraste inside.

Exeunt.

PRIDAMANT: Is that a stew,
Or isn't it?!

ALCANDRE: You panic easily.

PRIDAMANT: Then why not save him? Do some sorcery?

ALCANDRE: Sorcery's not required. Just have some patience:
Alarms will soon give way to celebrations.

END OF ACT THREE

ACT FOUR

Enter Isabelle.

ISABELLE: Love's lease, it seems, has all too short a date!
Tomorrow, my Clindor will learn his fate:
Tomorrow, an iniquitous decree
Will testify to blinkered tyranny –
Vengeance, disguised as justice, having tried
An act of self-defence as homicide
Will sentence him to death. Poor innocence!
So many powerful foes, such scant defence!
My father's hatred and his country's laws,
Combined with my cursed fate, are sealing yours!
Your only crimes, as far as I can see,
Were beauty, virtue, wit – and loving me!
For these, poor luckless wanderer, you die,
And so, love's reasoning dictates, must I:
My life is meaningless deprived of yours –
Your death demands my own – I was its cause.
A single moment joins our parting breaths:
Two amorous souls will reunite in death!
My father's cruelty, in the world beyond,
Its power reversed, confirms the sacred bond!
Then you must learn to mourn, inhuman father!
My love and I will mock your grief together:
Your tears will start to flow as we dry ours –
Our joy will be enhanced by your remorse.
But, lest remorse exact too low a cost,
You will be haunted daily by my ghost
In myriad shapes, that make you sick with fright,
Fluttering round you in the horrid night!
They'll bay for blood; beckon you after me;
Heap your declining years with misery;
Until at last you envy me my fate. . . .

Enter Lyse.

LYSE: Madame! What are you doing up this late?
What happens if your father finds you here?

ISABELLE: Ah, Lyse! When hope deserts us, so must fear:
Where should a woman grieve, if not the place

Where she has last beheld her lover's face?
I can recall him more distinctly here –
His image and his accents seem so clear
To my tormented mind!

LYSE: I can't quite see
The point of piling on the agony.

ISABELLE: In such a pass what else am I to do?

LYSE: Your suitors were amazing men, it's true,
But one's been killed and one's as good as dead,
So why not get them both out of your head?
There's men who knock them into a cocked hat –
Just look around. . . .

ISABELLE: How dare you talk like that?!

LYSE: But what'll it achieve, this grief of yours?
(Apart from ruining your looks, of course.)
You can lament – and he'll still lose his head –
Or hunt a richer, handsomer one instead!
What's more, I know the very man. . . .

ISABELLE: Be gone!

LYSE: All right, but you won't find a better one.

ISABELLE: You rub the wound, when you should try to heal it.

LYSE: I'm overjoyed, and why should I conceal it?

ISABELLE: Such callousness is hard to justify.

LYSE: Just wait until you've heard the reason why.

ISABELLE: Spare me your reasons.

LYSE: It concerns you too. . . .

ISABELLE: Speak of my love – that's all I ask of you.

LYSE: These "callous" brains of mine have done far more
Than all your floods of tears – they've saved Clindor.

ISABELLE: They've saved Clindor?! You've saved my lover?!

LYSE: Yes.
And you could hardly call that callousness.

ISABELLE: Where is he, then?!

LYSE: What I can do I've done:
You'll have to finish off what I've begun.
If you're prepared to follow him, that is.

ISABELLE: Prepared! My happiness depends on his:
I'll follow him to Hell and back.

LYSE: I see.
Looks like a serious case of love to me.
Pay close attention, and do as I say:
Without your help he'll never get away.
The place they've locked him up in being nearby,
I happen to have caught the gaoler's eye.
Now, once I've caught the eye, if I'm inclined
To reel it in, the heart's not far behind –
This one was no exception.

ISABELLE: *(Momentarily amused.)* Is that so?
And I, as usual, am the last to know.

LYSE: I had a shrewd idea you'd disapprove.
But I'm attempting to return his love,
Now that your sweetheart's in his tender care –
I'm mad for him, as far as he's aware –
And if we think the one we love loves us
It tends to make us more . . . solicitous
(If that's the word I want) – accordingly,
He'll do, well, almost anything for me –
He'd sacrifice himself, move heaven and earth,
But he's afraid it's more than his job's worth
To let out murderers. What I tell him is:
He'll never get another chance like this
To make his fortune – or to marry me:
"This 'murderer's a lord from Brittany,"
(Says I) "a very rich and powerful man
Who calls himself 'Monsieur de la Montagne'
(That's not his real name) – just you let him go
And follow him up north, with me in tow –
He'll make us rich and give us his protection –
Otherwise, all you'll get from *me*'s rejection."
He hesitates at this – makes some excuse –
Then he proposes to me – I refuse,
And off I flounce. He follows me. . . .

ISABELLE: *(Urgently)* And then?

LYSE: The whole absurd routine begins again!
But don't despair – this morning I went back:
He seemed depressed – I launched a fresh attack:
"They're going to execute him soon," I said,
"And he's no use to anybody dead!
It's up to you. . . ." "We'll need some money, though,"
Comes the reply. "It's a long way to go.
This 'lord' of yours has got no gold. . . ."

ISABELLE: But Lyse,
I'd have provided all necessities –
My pearls – my jewels – my clothes. . . .

LYSE: No need for that:
I soon found out what he was driving at –
He thought Clindor and I were – well, you know –
I soon informed him that it wasn't so.
Since then, his attitude's completely changed:
He's certain everything can be arranged –
He says the future's never looked so bright –
We're all of us to slip away tonight.

ISABELLE: Tonight! That's wonderful!

LYSE: So you can see,
There's not much doubt about my loyalty:
I've said I'll marry somebody with whom
The marriage bed'll seem more like the tomb!

ISABELLE: Oh, Lyse, if only. . . .

LYSE: Save your thanks. Get packed.
I want to see your cabinet ransacked –
Your father's, too – here, look, I stole his keys
While he was sleeping. *(Hands her keys.)*

ISABELLE: You come with me, Lyse.

LYSE: I don't think *that* would be a good idea:
We chatter so, the old man's bound to hear. *(Both giggle.)*

ISABELLE: I don't believe you're ever serious!

LYSE: There's no worse pair of prattlers than us!

They go into a noisy fit of giggling, then sshhh one another.

Joking apart, I have to wait down here

For our reluctant rescuer to appear.
We'll come and fetch you presently.

ISABELLE: All right –
I'll let you give the orders, for tonight –
(Leaving) Keep a close watch.

LYSE: *(Calling after her.)* And happy plundering!
(Alone) It's me you have to thank for everything,
Monsieur Clindor: I had you put in chains,
And only I can get you out again.
Revenge was what I wanted, and I got it –
I draw the line at seeing you garotted!
No, you can have your life – your pleasures, too –
Some self-restraint is all I want from you:
Remember that I've found another mate,
And try and be a bit less passionate:
(Becoming comically censorious.)
Your fancy shouldn't rule you – if you let it,
I'll tell my mistress and you'll soon regret it!

Isabelle re-enters in some agitation, followed by Matamore.

ISABELLE: What are you doing here?!

MATAMORE: The other day. . . .

ISABELLE: What are you after now? Please go away.

LYSE: *(To Isabelle.)* This crazy captain turns up everywhere!

ISABELLE: *(To Lyse.)* We bumped into each other on the stairs!

MATAMORE: . . . . when what I longed for was to share your bed,
I offered other services instead.

ISABELLE: What of it?

MATAMORE: In the skirmish you withdrew,
And I was bold enough to follow you –
In order to protect you. . . .

ISABELLE: Oh, I see –
An act of signal generosity.

MATAMORE: Since then your servant, beauteous Isabelle,
Has been an ever-watchful sentinel
Up in the topmost reaches of the house. . . .

LYSE: He means, he crept there like a frightened mouse.

MATAMORE: Frightened!

LYSE: You're shaking now – with fear, I'd say.

MATAMORE: I ride my fear – it speeds me on my way –
Invisible – the mind's Bucephalus –
Ever-obedient, ever-tremulous
Beneath me!

LYSE: A peculiar choice of mount!

ISABELLE: But did you leave your post on my account?

MATAMORE: I did – to bring your lover back: I mean
To smash those prison gates to smithereens;
To snap those adamantine chains. . . .

LYSE: What rot:
It's food he's left his "post" for, like as not.

ISABELLE: You've been there several days, you and your . . . horse –
What did you eat?

MATAMORE: Ambrosia. . . .

LYSE: Of course!
Nutritious stuff, that is!

MATAMORE: I've had my fill –
In fact, it's left me feeling rather ill.
The gods assure me that it does them good –
Personally, I prefer terrestrial food.

LYSE: Talk about fussy!

MATAMORE: Nectar, too, I find,
Can rot the teeth and causes chronic wind.
These being my circumstances, I'm afraid
Your larder suffered the occasional raid. . . .

ISABELLE: You mean to say you stole from us?!

MATAMORE: Madame,
You've seen what a hot-tempered man I am –
If you intend to. . . .

ISABELLE: Fetch the servants, Lyse.

MATAMORE: *(Running off.)* Only a fool awaits his enemies!

LYSE: *(With mock sadness.)* He's left you in the lurch.

ISABELLE: That horse of his
Just ran away with him!

They both laugh.

LYSE: Meanwhile, of course,
You won't have touched that cabinet of yours. . . .

ISABELLE: He stopped me – it was dark – I was alone –
There was no telling what he might have done –
Woken the house up, at the very least –
Rather than make a scene, I thought it best
To bring him here, and clearly I was right,
Since, with your help, the fiend's been put to flight.

LYSE: We've had some fun – we've also wasted time.

ISABELLE: I'll soon catch up. . . .

Enter Gaoler.

LYSE: It's him! Partners in crime,
That's what you are – if you're in any doubt
About him, now's the time to sound him out.

ISABELLE: *(To the gaoler, melodramatically.)*
What do you bring me? Life, or death? Dear friend,
My happiness, my fragile hopes, depend
On you.

GAOLER: *(Very blunt.)* Well, everything's been taken care of –
There are no obstacles that I'm aware of –
Horses are ready – we'll be safe away
In next to no time.

ISABELLE: How can one repay
Such services as these? What *is* it worth
To have a guardian angel here on earth?!

LYSE: His preparations may've been first rate,
But who's to get us through the northern gate?

GAOLER: No need for that – there's lots of places where
The walls have fallen into disrepair –
We'll slip away through one of those, and join
Our horses on the outskirts of the town.

ISABELLE: What joy can spring from such a brief reply!

GAOLER: Let's hurry. . . .

ISABELLE: We can leave immediately.
Come, Lyse, we'll each attack a cabinet!

Blackout.

The prison. Clindor, alone.

CLINDOR: Sweet memories, linger – don't desert me yet:
Who would have thought rehearsing you could bring
Such solace in the depths of suffering?
Blot out impending doom without a trace
And paint a brighter picture in its place –
Remind me, in the midst of my distress,
How little I deserved that happiness
I since have lost – chastise my aspiration
For venturing so far beyond my station –
Then, deeming death a fitting punishment
For my temerity, I'll die content. . . .
But oh, how bravely my imagination
Belies the horror of my situation!
If dying for her love ennobles me,
To lose the sight of her is purgatory:
The wretch who tried to kill me harms me more
Beyond the grave – his instrument, the law.
Avenging harpies, rising from his blood,
Bid public force take up the private feud:
I killed a man who would have cut me down,
But, since I am a stranger in this town,
It seems my courage and my innocence
Are crimes, and I'm condemned with no defence.
Justice succumbs to interest, and the state
Champions a murderer – a reprobate.
In his black name I must be sacrificed,
And, for avoiding death, death is the price.
How dire, and yet how drôle, the outcome seems –
What twisted thoughts – what terrifying dreams!
My visions have a gruesome clarity:
Death stands beside his grim machinery –
I face his agents in their black array –
Hear myself sentenced and am led away,
Dragging my irons, with the hoots and jeers
Of hostile townsfolk ringing in my ears,
To where the scaffold waits. I stare, distraught,

Incapable at last of rational thought –
Its consolation cannot reach me here –
Now face to face with death, half dead with fear!

Enter Gaoler.

GAOLER: Their worships have been thrashing out your case,
And justice has revealed its human face. . . .

CLINDOR: Heaven be thanked!

GAOLER: They'll do you in at night.

CLINDOR: And you call that humanity?

GAOLER: That's right.
You should be grateful, exiting this way –
It beats a public hanging any day!

CLINDOR: When death is something to be grateful for
I'll thank my judges and respect their law.

GAOLER: You're darnright lucky, if you only knew it.

CLINDOR: You've got a job to do – shut up and do it!

GAOLER: Follow me, then – the crossbowmen are waiting.

Enter Lyse and Isabelle.

ISABELLE: Where is he, Lyse?

LYSE: *(Aside)* She's almost palpitating!

ISABELLE: Our lives are now inseparably combined:
Our fates are one – the threads are intertwined!

GAOLER: When did you see a crossbowman like this?

CLINDOR: Have I escaped their bolts to die of bliss?
You scoundrel, you!

ISABELLE: Clindor!

CLINDOR: My love!
They kiss.

GAOLER: Stop this!
Once we've escaped we'll all have time to kiss.

CLINDOR: "*We'll all have time*"?! You mean. . . . ?

He looks at Lyse, highly amused.

ISABELLE: There's lots to tell. . . .

GAOLER: And lots of time to tell it in, as well,
Now, let's get on.

ISABELLE: All right. But look you two,
Before we leave, we want a pledge from you:
Until we're married, you must both contain
Your lust - or else, we'll head for home again.

CLINDOR: Don't think of it - you have my solemn word.

GAOLER: *(Grudgingly)* Mine, too.

LYSE: The prettiest pledge I ever heard!

Exeunt in high spirits.

ALCANDRE: Plucked from the jaws of suffering and disgrace,
For a long time pursued, but never traced,
Your son is safe.

PRIDAMANT: Then I can rest at last!

ALCANDRE: As we rejoin the tale, two years have passed.
From numerous trials, too lengthy to relate,
Our friends emerge in an exalted state,
As you shall see, when everything's arranged.
Our cast of phantom players must be changed:
Well though they have enacted these events
(Your fears bore witness to their excellence)
The following scenes require me to enlist
New spells and loftier protagonists.

They retire into the cave.

END OF ACT FOUR

ACT FIVE

The same.

ALCANDRE: Once more, stay close to me until you're told:
You've only death to gain by waxing bold.

Enter Isabelle, representing Hippolyte, and Lyse as Clarine.

PRIDAMANT: It's Isabelle! My, what a transformation!

ALCANDRE: Lyse follows, in a role to suit her station.

LYSE: Say, madam, wherefore is it your delight
In frosty bowers to while away the night?

ISABELLE: A secret grief, that by concealment grows,
To thee alone, Clarine, I shall disclose:
Prince Florilame. . . .

LYSE: Is absent – this I know.

ISABELLE: And from that very absence springs my woe!
The courtesy and love this prince has shown,
Bidding us use his gardens as our own,
Are mocked by my perfidious husband, for
'Tis here he dallies with his paramour,
Princess Rosine. But soon the wretch will find
I am not to be used in such a kind!

LYSE: The wisest women, whom this fate befell,
Feigned ignorance of what they knew too well:
For oft' our jealous shows – what least we meant –
Confirm our errant husbands in their bent.
Rail how we may, they are our masters still –
Then what can railing do but flesh their will?

ISABELLE: Must I then nurture the adult'rous flame?
His wife in substance she, and I in name?
Where men ride roughshod over Hymen's laws
Are women meekly to neglect His cause?

LYSE: Time was when men respected Hymen's vow,
Nor fear nor constancy control them now;
The empire waxes still – ours must contract –
Our honour's shattered, theirs remains intact;

Be true, was Hymen's teaching – History's is:
Measure men's honour by their mistresses!

SABELLE: Call it not honour, but mere vanity,
That can be swelled by infidelity:
If constancy's a blot on their good name,
'Tis ignominy men should seek, not fame.
Let constant husbands, censured everywhere,
With pride the stigma of their virtue bear:
Such upright renegades I shall revere.

LYSE: One's at the gate! Perchance your husband's here.

ISABELLE: Come, we'll withdraw and let him pass. . . .

LYSE: Too late:
He sees us. . . .

Clindor, representing Théagène, enters.

CLINDOR: *(To Isabelle.)* In the name of Cupid, wait!
Are these the sweets of love you promised me –
Now, when we should embrace, to turn and flee?
My wife's asleep, Prince Florilame's away –
Cupid himself doth counsel you to stay!

ISABELLE: *(Turning back and revealing herself.)*
Thy wife's awake. . . .

CLINDOR: *(Aside)* And Cupid is unkind!

ISABELLE: She sees her inj'ries, who before was blind:
In vain the sins of men eschew the light –
The eye of purity sees best by night!
And hast thou not proclaimed thine own transgression?
Adultery sits ill with indiscretion!
False wretch! Where are thy vows of constancy?
Or callst thou a twelvemonth eternity?
Say not thy star was loftier than mine –
My fortunes faltered, being conjoined with thine.
I was content in rags with thee to roam,
To cross my father and to quit my home,
To bear without complaint the blows of fate,
Ere chance did raise thee to this high estate.
But if thy faith is with thy fortunes changed,
That breast whence, for thy sake, I was estranged –

Restore me to it now, since willingly,
And in pure love, I braved the fates for thee!

CLINDOR: Is't then thy love thou wouldst arraign me for?
These charges should be laid at Cupid's door –
And at thine own, for tending Cupid's fire:
Not me thou follow'dst, but thine own desire.
I was a vagabond ere this, 'tis true,
But 'twas a state thy love inured thee to.
I wooed thee for thy fortune? 'Twas well done!
Thy fortune quit thee, e'en as thou wert won.
Love was thine only portion – mine a sword:
That danger brought, this raised me to a lord.
Bewail thy father and thy former life,
Though princes do thee honour as my wife;
Descant upon thy former riches still,
And call it famine when thou hast thy fill!
Know'st thou the touch of want, or of constraint?
How empty, then, must sound this new complaint:
Nor coldness canst thou tax me with, nor scorn –
Sure, women are the strangest creatures born!
For let us husbands serve them how we may
(As Cupid's hests do bend us to their sway);
Grant them whatever foolish thing they please;
Forego our own content to do them ease;
Yet trespass in this one respect – oh, then
We learn they'd have us live like saints, not men!
Well might you think, to hear them caterwaul,
Murder and rapine scarce were crimes at all;
Nor any vengeance fit for harmless sport,
Save that which Jove upon the Titans wrought!

ISABELLE: 'Twas not for glory I did follow thee:
I loved thee in despite of thy degree.
But if thou art thus hardened to my wrongs,
The duty, yet, that to this prince belongs
Dissuade thee from thy present course: 'twas he
Did, on such scant acquaintance, favour thee;
Gave thee the rank of captain, and did bring
Thy merits to the notice of his king.
Art grown thus rank? Feelst not what thou dost owe
To him that planted thee and watched thee grow?
He took such pains for thee that, at this hour,
Though less in blood, thou hast the greater power:

This brought down jibes and insults on his head –
And in return, thou wouldst defile his bed!
His goodness, thou with grossness dost repay;
What he hath not bestow'd, thou tak'st away!

CLINDOR: My soul – for 'tis the name I'll know thee by,
In spite of all, till one of us must die –
Can punishment, think'st thou, or death, dismay
A heart o'er which thy charms have lost their sway?
When thou dost call me ingrate, renegade,
Then, by thine own sweet lips, our love's betrayed:
A tyrant passion serve I, 'gainst my will,
Else wert thou mistress of my fancy still.
For Love thou wert content in rags to roam,
To cross thy father and to quit thy home –
'Tis this same god doth now usurp mine eyes
And means to rob thee of a brace of sighs.
Nay then, forgive, who know his power so well:
Thy place I'll lease a while, but never sell!
Only in virtue can Love's flower take root –
Sans which the merest frost were lethal to't:
Ours hath a vigour that shall never fail;
Age cannot wither it, nor custom stale
Its infinite variety! 'Twill last –
'Twill grow – till thou and I have breathed our last.
These foolish fancies quickly run their course:
Hers for a day, I am forever yours.

ISABELLE: *(Aside)* Alas! Against myself I do conspire:
My honour is at odds with my desire –
I love the author of my misery,
And still persuade myself that he loves me.
(To Clindor.)
When first a woman finds herself betrayed,
Unruly passions are perforce displayed,
Nor, in my jealous transports, canst thou see
Ought, but the tokens of my love for thee.
Forgive them then, as I must, in my turn,
O'erlook a flame that hath not long to burn.
Show me that wife whose beauty did not fade;
That husband whose affections never strayed:
How hast thou sinned, obeying Nature's law?
Only return to me – I ask no more.
Yet have a care, lest Hymen's anger bring

This dalliance to a bitter reckoning.
Too oft the loves of great ones are descried;
Envy is serpent-tongued and Argus-eyed:
If Florilame himself suspect thee not,
'Twill not be long, if ought of men I wot,
Ere some malicious courtier, fall'n from grace,
Seek, by denouncing thee, to get thy place.
Then must his wrath (ah, me! the Heav'ns forfend)
Like Jove's own bolt upon thy head descend!
Therefore be watchful, since thou art inclined
To pleasures of so perilous a kind;
Thy errors I condone, since err thou must,
But do not pawn thy life to pay thy lust!

CLINDOR: Alas, your ardent lovers are mere fools –
They laugh at death until their ardour cools!

ISABELLE: Embrace thy ruin, since it holds no fears –
Contemn thy fate, as thou dost scorn my tears!
And yet, thinkst thou this prince will be content
With so peremptory a punishment?
Thou being gone, thy wife – disgraced, alone –
Upon his doubtful mercy shall be thrown:
Then, if he be not sated with thy blood,
My innocence remains to make it good!
Thy fate is certain – must I then remain
To eke thy death out with a greater pain,
And, when thy shameful end hath not sufficed,
See my long-cherished honour sacrificed?
If this be all thou canst to me bequeath,
I'll scorn thy legacy and share thy death;
My body thine in death, as 'twas in life –
No ravisher shall ever touch thy wife!
Such is my destiny – forever thine –
Never thy mistress' husband's concubine!
Farewell, I'll run before thee to that goal,
Release thee from thy vows and save thy soul!

CLINDOR: Beloved wife, live on, if but to see
The wond'rous change thy virtue makes in me:
Faithful to him that wrongs thee, glad to die
But on a doubt of what my foes may try –
Such courage and such constancy thou show'st,
In sooth, I know not which I prize the most,

But these, conjoined, have brought me 'neath thy sway
And hold my lusts, like ravening beasts, at bay.
For these my sickly and imprisoned soul
Leaps, laughing, from its fetters and is whole.
I know not, by what subtle arts beguiled. . . .

ISABELLE: 'Tis all forgot, and we are reconciled.

CLINDOR: Though all terrestrial beauties should conspire
To subjugate me to some fresh desire,
Proof against their assaults, my heart shall own
The empire of this goddess' eyes alone!

Enter the Gaoler, representing Eraste, with servants of Prince Florilame, who apprehend Clindor.

ERASTE: Rejoice, thou traitor, and receive from me
This favour, that thy mistress sends to thee!

He runs Clindor through.

PRIDAMANT: *(To Alcandre.)*
He's killing him! And you're not helping! Why?

ERASTE: And thus may foul seducers ever die!

ISABELLE: Butcher! What make you here?

ERASTE: I strike this blow,
That generations yet unborn may know
The price of treachery – never so abhorred
As in the churl who turns against his lord.
He wronged Prince Florilame, his wife and you:
Thus, to all three, this sacrifice is due;
Rejoice in your unworthy husband's end,
Nor scorn a champion you should commend!

Exit Eraste. The domestics remain.

ISABELLE: And yet he hath but died in moiety:
Come, kill the rest – for he lives on in me!
My doubtful heart, inspired yet impotent,
This blow foresaw, though it could not prevent:
Our prescience mocks itself, when what we see
Comes nonetheless, with dire calamity!
If. . . . But alas, with bitter cares oppressed,
My soul slips, piecemeal, from my panting breast;

Then welcome, death – my comfort lies in this:
E'en as it slips away, 'tis joining his. . . .

LYSE: Madam? Alas, her final throes begin –
I'll say no more, but seek for aid within.

Lyse exits and a curtain descends, concealing the garden and the bodies of Clindor and Isabelle. Alcandre and Pridamant leave the cave.

ALCANDRE: Our hopes are tiny Ixions, tightly bound
On Fortune's wheel – they rise as it goes round
And fall again – we scale her topmost height
Only to plunge into some ghastly plight.

PRIDAMANT: What consolation can a father draw,
In such a crisis, from so bland a saw?
It's not as if a lapdog's breathed its last!
My son's been murdered, and all hope is past!
You needn't try consoling me – instead
I'll look for death, since what I lived for's dead.

ALCANDRE: I can quite sympathise with your despair;
As for consoling you – I wouldn't dare:
If you're intent on following him, go.
But can you trust your hand to strike the blow?
Grief should suffice, if fed with grievous sights,
As, for example, Clindor's funeral rites. . . .

At this point the curtain is raised again, to reveal the actors sharing out the night's takings.

PRIDAMANT: Even the dead, it seems, count up their pence!

ALCANDRE: He counts his with a certain negligence. . . .

PRIDAMANT: I don't believe it! Yet more prodigies!
My son, his murderers, his wife and Lyse!
Some instant charm has ended all dispute,
And mixed the living with the dead, to boot!

ALCANDRE: Like any actors, following the play
They reassemble to sort out their pay.
One thrusts, another falls, a third laments,
But plot dictates the pattern of events:
Conflict and death flow from the poet's pen –
The curtain falls, and all are friends again.
Your son and his companions, so astute

In slipping off and foiling all pursuit,
Found freedom less rewarding than they'd thought,
And took up acting as a last resort.

PRIDAMANT: My son . . . an actor!

ALCANDRE: Not just him – all four.
What you've just seen – his clandestine amour
And bloody end – conclude a tragedy
That was presented by his company
Tonight, in Paris. It appears they've had
Quite a success – the audience went mad!
Hence all the gold. As for that fine array –
You may perhaps recall my first display –
It *is* worn by your son, whom it affords
A borrowed grandeur while he struts the boards.

PRIDAMANT: Deceived again! So this is what you meant
By speaking of him as magnificent,
And this is fortune's "topmost height" – THE STAGE!
I'd rather he was dead!

ALCANDRE: Control your rage:
The theatre's a prestigious field these days –
What your day scorned, the present heaps with praise –
Tomorrow, country folk will gladly pay
For what the Paris wits applaud today –
Actors are virtual demi-gods, adored
Alike by prince and pauper, lout and lord.
Where do you think the statesman now repairs,
Anxious and weary with the nation's cares?
He buys a ticket for the latest play,
Where all those weighty matters melt away.
The king himself, less man than meteor,
A Jupiter in peace, a Mars in war,
Whose laurel crown proclaims his awesome power,
From time to time will pass a carefree hour
At the *Théâtre français*. Parnassus there
Unfolds its many marvels, rich and rare,
And there the greatest scholars often choose
To spend an evening with their favourite muse.
Besides, if wealth is what you're looking for,
Few occupations these days offer more:
Your son, for one, has done far better there

Than in his father's none-too-tender care!
In short, you have no reason to complain –
It's brought him status and financial gain.

PRIDAMANT: I shan't complain again – in fact, you've shown
That his profession's nobler than my own.
My anger sprang from preconceived ideas
About the theatre that I've held for years,
Ignoring its utility and charm –
Such criticisms your remarks disarm.
He has done well!

ALCANDRE: Then you believe your eyes?

PRIDAMANT: I'm setting out for Paris at sunrise.
To you – the great Alcandre – I owe all this,
Yet how can one repay such services?

ALCANDRE: Assisting men of honour is my trade:
If you're content, I count myself well paid.

PRIDAMANT: What value can be placed on your advice?
I shall remember you – that must suffice.

THE END